The Architecture of Participation

INSUBORDINATIONS: ITALIAN RADICAL THOUGHT
Lorenzo Chiesa, series editor

1. *The Monopoly of Man,* Anna Kuliscioff
2. *Convention and Materialism: Uniqueness without Aura,* Paolo Virno
3. *On Freud,* Elvio Fachinelli
4. *Italian Operaismo: Genealogy, History, Method,* Gigi Roggero
5. *The Morals of Life: Biology, Biopolitics, Bioethics,* Davide Tarizzo
6. *The Architecture of Participation,* Giancarlo De Carlo

The Architecture of Participation

Giancarlo De Carlo

introduction by Luisa Lorenza Corna

translated by Alex Fletcher and Elisa Adami

The MIT Press / Cambridge, Massachusetts / London, England

The MIT Press
Massachusetts Institute of Technology
77 Massachusetts Avenue
Cambridge, MA 02139
mitpress.mit.edu

The translation of this work has been funded by SEPS
Segretariato Europeo per le Pubblicazioni Scientifiche

SEPS
SEGRETARIATO EUROPEO PER LE PUBBLICAZIONI SCIENTIFICHE

The MIT Press would like to thank the anonymous peer reviewers who provided comments on drafts of this book. The generous work of academic experts is essential for establishing the authority and quality of our publications. We acknowledge with gratitude the contributions of these otherwise uncredited readers.

This book was set in Bebas Neue Pro and Arnhem Pro by Westchester Publishing Services. Printed and bound in the United States of America.

Library of Congress Cataloging-in-Publication Data

Names: Fletcher, Alex translator | Adami, Elisa translator | Corna, Luisa Lorenza writer of introduction | De Carlo, Giancarlo, 1919-2005 Architettura della partecipazione. English | De Carlo, Giancarlo, 1919-2005 Piramide rovesciata. English
Title: The architecture of participation / Giancarlo De Carlo; introduction by Luisa Lorenza Corna ; translated by Alex Fletcher and Elisa Adami.
Description: Cambridge, Massachusetts : The MIT Press, [2026] | Series: Insubordinations: Italian radical thought | Includes bibliographical references.
Identifiers: LCCN 2025027841 (print) | LCCN 2025027842 (ebook) | ISBN 9780262052689 paperback | ISBN 9780262052696 pdf | ISBN 9780262052702 epub
Subjects: LCSH: Architecture and society | Architecture—Study and teaching
Classification: LCC NA2543.S6 D34 2026 (print) | LCC NA2543.S6 (ebook)
LC record available at https://lccn.loc.gov/2025027841
LC ebook record available at https://lccn.loc.gov/2025027842

EU Authorised Representative: Easy Access System Europe, Mustamäe tee 50, 10621 Tallinn, Estonia | Email: gpsr.requests@easproject.com

Contents

Contents

Series Foreword

Insubordinations are creative and innovative double negations. They occur when an existing negative condition, the state of being "sub" or "under" a given order and thereby having an inferior rank, is countered by negating this very subjection. In our current late-capitalist predicament such a reversal acquires a more complex meaning. The ordering authority is in fact no longer simply in crisis and exposed to resistance but profoundly disordered in its own operative structure. Today, powers traditionally devoted to regulation perpetuate and reinforce their effectiveness by continually deregulating themselves. Orders become more and more oppressive precisely as they unveil the inconsistency on which they rest. As Pier Paolo Pasolini presciently put it almost fifty years ago, by now, "nothing is more anarchic than power." In this desolate scenario, actual insubordination cannot but arise as the tentative search for a *new* kind of order. Its long-term and admittedly ambitious mission is the establishment of a society without subordinates, called "communism." Its first and more realistic task is a taxonomic critique of an Order that resolves itself into myriad conflicting, yet no less tyrannical, suborders.

The present series aims to dissect the contemporary variant of the double negation involved in insubordination through the privileged prism of Italian radical thought. Starting from the late 1970s, Italy emerged as a laboratory for test-piloting the administration of the state of exception we are now living on a planetary level, both geopolitically and in our everyday lives. A brutal repression put an abrupt end to an intense season of social and political emancipations. But the theoretical elaboration of that defeat, which should not be confused with a grieving process, has managed to promote Italian radical thought to the center of a series of international debates that endeavor to define a new function and field of revolutionary politics. The series moves from the assumption that while so-called Italian Theory remains a vague and awkward category and attempts at hegemonizing it run the risk of resurrecting the idea of a national philosophy, it is beyond doubt that a growing number of left-wing Italian authors have, for good reasons, become very popular worldwide.

Drawing on philosophy, political theory, psychoanalysis, architecture, art history, anthropology, sociology, economics, and other fields, this interdisciplinary series intends to both further investigate consolidated Italian theories of emancipation and introduce authors (both present and past) who still remain largely unknown among Anglophone readers. Insubordinations: Radical Italian Thought will also foster original critical readings that pinpoint the tensions inherent to the oeuvre of prominent progressive thinkers and develop novel dialogues with various strands of post–World War II militant thought (such as heterodox Marxism, biopolitical theory, feminism of difference, social psychoanalysis, anti-psychiatry, and theories of Fascism). The series will also translate works by seminal earlier Italian authors who may be regarded as "forerunners" or critics *avant la lettre* of current trends in Italian radical thought.

It is my hope that, by delving into the titles of this series, readers will be able to appreciate the disciplined indiscipline they all share.

Lorenzo Chiesa

Architecture of Reversal

The neoliberal turn of most contemporary democracies has been putting pressure on the values that sustained Western higher education, ultimately causing a restructuring of its "deputed form."[1] This restructuring varied depending on context, as universities operate within specific cultural traditions and maintain different relationships to their respective states.[2] Whereas post–9/11 American academia, for example, has been experiencing a curtailing of its freedom both through muscular state interventions and more subtle practices of containment and censorship, British universities have become the target of draconian cuts, casualizations, and qualitative evaluations, which have in turn, prompted a swirl of staff resistance.[3] More shielded by the state from violent neoliberal restructuring, continental countries, like Italy or Germany, are nonetheless mimicking the UK and American models, for instance, by prompting academics to enter competitive grant schemes, in the (delusional) attempt to shackle their provincial and nepotistic logic.

The university as a battleground is, however, not a novelty of the early twenty-first century. In the collective memory of the educated middle class, the 1970s still evoke university occupations and their zestful utopian impetus, marked by creative slogans against the institution and its allies amid the academic body. Yet, fifty years later, the roles in the struggles have been reshuffled, with members of staff moving to the forefront of mobilizations to protect their jobs and students receding to the background. Often students express solidarity with members of staff, but the raising of fees and their own transformation into "consumers" inevitably complicates the possibility of lasting alliances between the two.

* * *

The pamphlet *The Overturned Pyramid*, which opens this edited collection, stands oddly in defiance of the historical trajectory drafted earlier. It represents one of the rare accounts of 1960s students' unrest narrated from the viewpoint of an academic in solidarity with the protesters.[4] If the optics don't suffice to question the official version of events, they certainly shed a new light on the dynamics of power shaping the postwar university in Italy with their excessively polarized accounts. De Carlo always chose the students over the academics, but his granular analysis of university hierarchies and curriculum design painted a picture of institutional power as diffuse, hardly graspable, and extremely viscous. The text occupies a middle ground between Marx and Foucault, for while it clings to a bipartite structure of power, it posits its very source as unfathomable.

If we shift our perspective from *The Overturned Pyramid* to our present time, we may be drawn to a different set of concerns. Rather than focusing on De Carlo's critique of academic hierarchies, our attention turns to his effort to align with the "other part," while remaining acutely aware of his own distinct position. This awareness, at times, gives rise to a sympathetic critique of the students' class role and their tactics. De Carlo's lesson for our riven present is that only a convergence of struggles can *overthrow* the contemporary academic *pyramid*, yet in looking for the demands that unite students and academics, it's crucial to acknowledge that neoliberalism has set us apart.

* * *

In 1968, the year of the pamphlet's publication, De Carlo was an established architect and a pedagogue with several years of teaching experience in Italy and abroad. Between 1963 and 1967, he taught urban planning at the University of Venice, and in 1966, he was visiting lecturer at the faculty of architecture of Yale University. In the following year he was called to coordinate a design studio at MIT, and he started his collaboration with the Polytechnic of Milan. As Filippo de Pieri observes in his preface to the 2018 republication of *La piramide rovesciata*, parallels can be gleaned between De Carlo's seminars at the Polytechnic and the concerns that would be soon raised by the academics and students there. Run in collaboration with architect Paolo Ceccarelli, the seminars sought to debunk the presumed neutrality of urban planning and encourage students to devise proposals that turned that discipline on its head, subverting its economic priorities.[5]

While trying to change architecture through a revision of course contents, student protests intensified, ultimately leading to the occupation of universities. De Carlo doesn't step back. He decides to get involved and register the unfolding events. Asked to take part in an itinerant program of public talks across the country in February 1968, De Carlo delivers a speech on the students' upheaval at the Milan Polytechnic.[6] A couple of months later, a revised version of the talk, supplemented with an appendix of documents, is sent off for printing. De Carlo is in a hurry. A few students' documents are missing, but he exhorts the publisher to go ahead, "since we are in the right moment, and everything is changing rapidly."[7]

* * *

The publication of *The Overturned Pyramid* coincided with a specific historical moment, both nationally and internationally. The occupation of Italian universities was, in fact, preceded and paralleled by an expansion in the scope and scale of higher education, with the US playing a pioneering role and most industrialized countries of the global north following suit. Behind the educational boom was the growth of industrial capitalism, which generated a demand for the training of an expanding workforce and a competition between states enhanced by the Cold War. As historian Tom Holert highlights, the gargantuan Western investment in education and research was partly a compensatory reaction to a feeling of scientific belatedness caused by the successful launch of *Sputnik*.[8]

The centrality of higher education in the economic and political agenda of Western states found correspondence in the realm of architecture. The increasing number of students required new and more capacious buildings, prompting the architectural industry to respond. A brief examination of the main professional journals of the time testifies to this booming field. In 1968, the British *AD*, the American *Progressive Architecture*, and the French *L'architecture aujourd'hui* dedicated special issues to the design of university buildings. Their pages are filled with plans and detailed views of upcoming campuses, as well as speculative debates about the "university of the future." Compounding sketches and written reflections, the contributors imagined how new technological devices and higher mobility could revolutionize educational architecture.

Significant, in this respect, was Cedric Price's contribution to the May 1968 issue of *AD*, for which he acted as a guest editor. Here, the British architect presented *Atom*, an educational project that replaced single or comprehensive physical units with buildings made of "kits of [mobile] parts." The project responded to the increasing fragmentation of human life and the need to disenfranchise education from "particular requirements made by any particular authority."[9] Along similar lines, texts by architects Michael Pearson, John E. Tirrell, and Albert A. Canfield announced a "goodbye to the classroom," envisioning students scattered throughout open spaces and connected by synchronized closed-circuit televisions.[10] Techno-fetishism loomed large in both the American and British surveys. New devices would allow administrators, we read in *PA*, "to individualise the learning process," a term used in a positive sense as a synonym of a rhetoric of flexibility and freedom.[11] And the superseding of schools' physical limits was believed to effect, seamlessly, a dissolution of the "natural barriers to cultural exchange between peoples."[12] The architectural community appeared eager to embrace the new possibilities offered by technologies for rethinking contemporary schools and enthusiastically endorsed the new central role granted to education in social and economic planning.[13]

* * *

In the realm of architecture and education, Italy held a distinctively asynchronous position compared to its British and American counterparts. While industry and architecture magazines addressed the issue of university design at a later stage, architectural faculties took the lead in the wake of student uprisings. Few know that the surge of occupations in Italy began at the architecture faculty of the University of Venice as early as 1958, when the students blocked access to the building in response to the introduction of state examination. For De Carlo, architecture's purported "vanguard" role in the history of occupations wasn't a sign of students' distinctive disobedience but rather of a certain "belatedness" of the discipline. The delay was attributable to the discipline's position, caught between expressive ambitions and vocational imperatives, the opening of architectural faculties to a wider demographic and the establishment of examinations regulating eligibility for professional registration.[14]

These are some of the reasons that precipitated the occupation of the Milan Polytechnic. Initial disturbances commenced in January 1963, when a group of students penned a letter to the faculty members condemning the use of traditional teaching methods and the established governing system. They demanded a comprehensive modernization of the faculty, calling for greater inclusion of students in decision-making processes and encouraging staff to critically assess chosen themes and methods.[15] Photographs of the occupations taken by architectural student Walter Barbero show banners targeting professorial conservativism through a satirical use of premodern architectural elements.[16]

One features a drawing of a Doric capital alongside the scathing statement, "Incompetence and reaction are clearly manifested." Another contrasts Le Corbusier's visionary chapel in Ronchamp to the colonnade found in one of the faculty professor's designs. Protests, exam strikes, and self-managed workshops persisted until 1967, when the minister of education issued a circular authorizing "experimental teaching" in an effort to quell the ongoing unrest among students. By the end of the first year of pedagogical experimentation,[17] De Carlo published *The Overturned Pyramid*.

* * *

The pamphlet opens with a critical account of the history of Italian universities, beginning with the country's unification in the mid-nineteenth century and continuing with the Fascist educational reforms, whose effects continued to loom in the present. In the second part, the focus shifts to the events of the Polytechnic, providing a detailed description of the students' efforts to reform the institution and the academy's reaction. Finally, De Carlo concludes with proposal for an alternative educational model that responds to the emerging demands of the "mass university." Interestingly, the pamphlet contains no reference to the design and use of school buildings, thereby departing from the focus on architectural solutions and technological fixes found in the previously examined articles.[18] Space is present here in a different way, both as a method and a metaphor for interpreting university institutions. Evoking the title, for instance, the initial section views the university through the image of a pyramid, where a fundamental division separates those who possess "knowledge" (academics) from those who don't (students). But as the text progresses, the pyramid shifts from a simple metaphor for hierarchy to a complex geometric figure that De Carlo uses to represent a more intricate power structure. The text states:

> Another series of barriers hermetically divides the lecturers. There are voluntary assistants, tenured assistants, adjuncts, visiting professors, tenured professors, institute directors, deans, rectors. Here the barriers are horizontal, and their stratifications give rise to a pyramid whose edges vanish at the top into a dark band. An external observer judging their convergence might imagine the pyramid's apex to be close and concrete; but, in reality, the apex is not there. Beyond the dark and indecipherable band, the edges diverge and, shooting off in different directions, enter the tangled structure of the State. It is here, where the most unpredictable convergences and plots take place, that the University finds its most covert and indissoluble links with the system.[19]

As the description moves into finer details, the overarching contour of the pyramid and the connections between its various parts begins to blur. At this point, it becomes apparent that the spatial metaphor is not intended to enhance clarity, but to convey the sense of labyrinthine chaos experienced by all who inhabit academia. The neat distinction between staff and students described at the outset no longer holds, as the institution and its rules prove opaque, even to those at its upper echelons. These figures are drawn into a never-ending bidding game, for the pyramid in question lacks a clear vertex, or rather, its apex merges with the structure of the state, transforming the university into its ideological appendage. Here, Althusser's famous conceptualization of education as an ideological state apparatus comes to mind, but if we view it from a contemporary perspective, the same pyramidal structure may appear an anticipation of contemporary neoliberal organizations. In these settings, individuals engage in a life pattern of successive projects, continually enhancing their own "employability" as a form of "personal capital," which never finds a definite recognition or position.

Later in the text, De Carlo returns to spatial thinking to address the growth of the mass university. His stance on the theme is one of endorsement. Rather than a threat to the integrity of architectural education, the mass university is viewed as an opportunity to shake up its elitist foundations, turning the discipline into a structural necessity. He envisions this goal being pursued first by redesigning the faculty curriculum to allow greater flexibility between subjects and departments, and ultimately by fostering a more porous relationship between the academy and the city. In the text, we read:

> The departments break the traditional separation of subjects and establish a real unity of teaching by anchoring it to a flexible interplay of different cultural tensions, rather than a static

and predetermined configuration. These different tensions are encouraged to converge by the internal logic of the whole and by external stimuli coming from the social context.[20]

We may be tempted to link back De Carlo's interest in "flexibility" to Archigram's work, but if we want to get a comprehensive view on this, then international influences have to be read alongside national history and De Carlo's distinct political biography be brought to the fore. De Carlo wasn't just an *engaged architect* like others. He was, long before becoming a practicing architect, a "professional militant." With the aim of opposing and overthrowing the Italian fascist regime, in 1943, he joined partisan resistance in Northern Italy, living between Milan and the mountains around Lake Como.

The partisan years, he recalls later in an interview, were a thoroughly transformative moment, where the commitment to present struggle for the future liberation of the country had to go hand in hand with attempts to practice other ways of thinking and living *in the present*. During his extended sojourns in the mountains, following the evening meetings, De Carlo would often share his insights on modernist architecture with his comrades and explain how the ostentatious academic style that emerged during Mussolini's government correlated to its ideological agenda. Other comrades might talk about literature, art, music, or quantum physics. For him, these moments were crucial in shaping a new political subjectivity, as partisans needed to experience and understand "the whole spectrum of freedom."[21]

The leadership of the unit he was part of saw this activity as an unnecessary distraction from the primary goal of the struggle and swiftly put an end to it. The episode played a crucial importance in readjusting De Carlo's political belief and moving him away from party politics. In 1945, while most of his comrades decided to join the Italian Communist Party, he drifted toward anarchism and engaged with the work of Bakunin and Kropotkin.[22] That same year, he participated in the first Italian anarchist meeting, which he later praised for its openness in decision-making and its rejection of any concept of democracy based on majority rule. The possibility of finding agreement in disagreements, and of politics as a *choice of the means* explored in this context, will inform, to his own admission, his professional ethos in the following decade.[23] From this perspective, De Carlo's preference for scattered architectural structures may seem less closely related to Price's "kits of parts" and more akin to the long-standing aversion to political hierarchies, which had already emerged during his early political years. The same can be said, perhaps, of the "flexible" structure he envisions for mass universities. While his project may draw inspiration from open-plan classrooms as depicted in American and British magazines, it also appears to align with anarchist theories of spontaneous order and bottom-up organizing.

* * *

A proviso must be added here: De Carlo's anarchism was unorthodox from the outset. His interest in the theories of Bakunin and Kropotkin never translated into an endorsement of the communitarianism and small-group politics traditionally associated with this political tradition. The industrialization of Italy, accompanied by fast-paced urbanization and the expansion of the student population, demanded architects adopt a mindset of "big-scale thinking" and be receptive to its challenges. We have just seen this position articulated in the *Overturned Pyramid*, in passages where De Carlo expresses hope in the mass university, but it is worth examining another work from the same year, where his interest in large-scale planning intersects with university reforms and students' upheaval.

The year 1968 was a pivotal one for De Carlo. Not only did he publish two important books on higher education and architecture,[24] but he also assumed the role of director for the XIV Milan Triennial, Italy's foremost institution for design and contemporary culture. The tradition demanded that each nominated director would organize a thematic exhibition where the world's most innovative architects and designers would present their work upon invitation. De Carlo titled "his" show *The Big Number*, seemingly leveraging on its generic nature to evoke both attention and distress. The event asked architects and designers to respond to the quantitative leap in scale brought about by the new society, critically acting within this irreversible shift rather than conforming to capitalist pressures.

National and international contributors such as Alison and Peter Smithson, Arata Isozaki, Archigram, and Saul Bass crafted projects and installations exploring the challenges posed by population growth, alongside the corresponding expansion of infrastructural networks, housing, and communication systems. The exhibition stood out for its ambitious scope, both in terms of its form and content. While it departed from a merely descriptive approach to the theme by engaging in critical analysis, the display also defied the formal constraints of architecture, blending different types of media and languages.

Alongside individual contributors, the exhibition featured an introductory section co-curated by De Carlo,[25] which explored the "big number" through the key concepts of "errors," "information," and "perspectives." The opening segment, focusing on "error," launched a vigorous critique of the architectural establishment and the broader political class. This was conveyed through a display of images depicting alarming scenarios, printed on a suspended sicofoil ribbon that hung from the ceiling. The exhibition then moved to the "information" section, a vast reticular installation covered with banners presenting data and infographics about contemporary society. Its modular structure created the illusion of infinite extension, effectively dramatizing the overwhelming influx of information facilitated by the recent expansion of mass media. The final section, "perspectives" struck a hopeful tone: megaphones scattered throughout the space broadcasted positive messages about the future, while a totemic electronic calculator visualized the rapid passing of time.

Viewed with hindsight, the optimistic conclusion appears ironic in light of subsequent events. Known in history as "the Triennale lasting one day," the 1968 edition was occupied immediately following its inauguration. A photograph by Cesare Colombo shows a young De Carlo surrounded by students. He is standing amid the crowd, listening to one of the demonstrators with an attentive, tense expression.[26] Secondary literature on the events recounts De Carlo's efforts to stage a dialogue with a group of students determined to target a national symbol of cultural elitism. The efforts were unsuccessful, though, as the students broke into the exhibition space, spraying slogans on the building walls or directly on the installations. On a big white screen, we read: "Today, imagination, phantasy and revolution have buried reactionary forces."[27] The "burying" lasted a little more than a day; a week after the upheaval, the police, with the Triennial board's complicity, decided to evict the exhibition's occupiers. De Carlo resigned and distanced himself from state intervention.

In describing the show, I have omitted one crucial part: a room containing an installation designed by De Carlo himself, with filmmaker Marco Bellocchio and artist Bruno Caruso. It is worth briefly pausing on this installation as it stands out distinctly from the rest of the show, almost as if it was added afterward or left unresolved by its overarching concept and design. Titled *The Youth Protest* (*La protesta dei giovani*), the installation captures the spirit of international student unrest through an immersive design that urged viewers to confront the scene and take a stance.

Upon entering, visitors encountered a mountain of cobblestones, seemingly excavated from the streets, piled alongside broken kitchen appliances and an overturned van. Behind the debris, a large-scale photographic mural depicted students marching with banners, their images magnified to amplify their presence and intensify their voices. While the initial effect may have been one of immersion, the specific staging compelled visitors to take a position, literally placing them on the other side of the barricade, behind a heap of urban wreckage. Through this deliberate design, the installation moved beyond a mediated, educational intent, confronting the public directly and implicitly casting them in the role of counterrevolutionaries.

In reevaluating the events surrounding the XIV Milan Triennial, architect Paola Nicolin underscores the significance of the show's relationship to its historical context. She asks whether the idea of the exhibition as a platform for critique may have paved the way for the protest, suggesting that the occupation and vandalism of the space could be seen as a "phenomenological form" of De Carlo's curatorial vision.[28] This perspective is particularly relevant when considering *The Youth Protest*. Rather than interpreting the installation solely within the context of the exhibition curatorship I propose examining it from the standpoint of its subsequent occupation. Doing so reveals the room not merely as a reflection of external events but as a call to protesters, hoping their actions would animate the installation and challenge the art space. Seen in this light, *The Youth Protest* becomes evidence of De Carlo's complex, in-between position: caught between the inside and outside of the institution, between the limits of the architectural profession and the open field of the city. This position would go on to define his whole career.

Soon after occupation of the Triennale, De Carlo was asked to comment on the sequence of events by the left-wing newspaper *L'Unità*. While he remained firm in his opposition to the eviction and police violence, he did not spare criticism of the students, whom he saw as unable to turn the occupation into effective political action. Defying what one might expect from someone holding an institutional role such as director of the Triennale, his critique was not aimed at the students' uncompromising stance but rather at the narrow scope of their intervention, which he regarded as overly focused on striking a symbolic target rather than addressing the deeper foundations of cultural institutions. [29] The problem, once again, was that of scale. If the "big number" was the number of the future, critical endeavors had to measure up to those proportions.

* * *

Surprisingly, De Carlo's retrospective analysis of the occupation overlooks an aspect that closely aligns with his own ideas about architecture and politics. The assault on the Milan Triennial marked the first instance of students moving beyond the university campus to occupy a noneducational building in the city center. In retracing the protest movement that emerged at the Polytechnic of Milan, academic Lucia Tenconi highlights the growing entanglement between the university and its surrounding urban fabric—an evolving relationship, she explains, that operated in two directions.[30] If, in 1968, the impulse was to occupy an external institution to broaden the reach of the students' battle, a couple of years later, the university began hosting a group of families who had been evicted from council flats. In response, the students allowed this event to inform their teaching, running a thematic seminar on the housing problem until a solution to the displacement was found. This dual movement—of the students toward the city and, conversely, of the city toward the students' designated headquarters—suggests that the protests had, in some respects, succeeded in breaking or at least unsettling the corralled structure of higher education pedagogy. Equally, it indicates a broadening of the students' perspective over the course of the struggle. If the initial goal was to topple the remnants of the fascist system in higher education, from 1968 onward, the focus shifted to raising the bar, questioning the social mandate of the architectural profession at large, but also the purpose of the university in society.

* * *

These and other issues are addressed by De Carlo in his 1969 "Why/How to Build School Buildings."[31] Initially published in English and later in Italian, the text can be considered a sequel to *The Overturned Pyramid* and his experience with university occupations. The broadening of De Carlo's inquiry is already evident in the title, where the formal question ("how") is juxtaposed, if not sidelined, by a more far-reaching one, presaging a thorough interrogation of the very raison d'être of university buildings and their designers. These latter are, not surprisingly, absent in the photographs accompanying the article, which centers, instead, on students' gathering in public space. The sequence of images demands some attention.

The article begins with an 1895 photograph of a male-only class in uniforms, posed neatly and orderly in front of the camera. A few pages later, we are thrust into the streets of late 1960s Milan. Here, students march in mass, holding banners or each other's arms, seemingly chanting or shouting. In the background, we catch glimpses of the city's main landmarks, encircled by the crowd. Another image shows students climbing a monument, nearly engulfing it with their arms and legs. The final image, however, strikes a different tone. The scene is ambiguous: Two vans are parked in front of a building, three policemen stand looking in various directions, and three figures (possibly students) are seen from behind, but there is no event tying them together, no focal point to guide our gaze. On closer inspection, however, one can glimpse a man holding a camera at the back. He appears to be adjusting his photographic device, probably setting the exposure, checking the focus, or ensuring the film is running smoothly.

Placed alongside the 1895 photograph of students in uniforms, this image serves as both a circular conclusion and a radical reversal. The presence of the police can be interpreted as a warning of the risk of a "*retour à la normale*," as famously written on a May 1968 poster, while the chaotic composition reflects the disruption of social order incited by the students. Meanwhile, the man with the camera in the background underscores the media's role in covering the uprising. The students have taken to the streets, making headlines on the front pages of every newspaper. Relevant, in this regard, is the following sentence from the final section of the article:

> Newspaper photographs showing the events of the student revolt all over the world have revealed a new kind of school architecture that no architect nor educator had so far imagined.[32]

De Carlo experienced the unfolding of the students' revolt from within, but he also examined their *representations.* Photographs enable him to scrutinize how the students gather and disperse throughout the city, inhabit the streets, and contravene urban codes appropriating buildings or monuments. His idea of "a new educational architecture" departs from the focus on school building projects showcased in architectural journals and instead places the actions of the students at the center. The aim is to dislodge the "educational problem" from the narrow confines of the architectural discipline and reposition it within the much broader debate over the contemporary city and its social relations.

* * *

This shift must be understood in conjunction with architecture's departure from a focus on physical objects in the 1960s, and the expansion of the architect's role to encompass activities geared toward less tangible outcomes, such as spatial analysis, planning and performance. The 1960s also saw the city gaining a new centrality, as object of theoretical analysis and as a new scale for design interventions with the emerging of urban planning as a distinct discipline. These latter either took the forms of techno-optimistic fantasies such as those by Cedric Price, or of discrete, grassroots actions, initiated by committees of activist planners with local citizens. Further, those years coincided with the emerging of the city as *platform for learning*. A couple of publications marked this shift: the 1971 special issue of *Design Quarterly*, "Making the City Observable,"[33] edited by Richard Saul Wurman, and the release of *Streetwork: The Exploding School*[34] by Anthony Fysons and Colin Ward. While Wurman's issue pioneered new ways of decoding contemporary cityscape through mapping and infographics, Fysons and Ward's prompted architectural teachers and students to venture beyond the confines of the classroom and explore the city as an expansive pedagogical environment.[35]

We can certainly position De Carlo's 1969 text within this line of enquiry, but this should be done with a few aspects in mind that set his work apart. Ward's and Wurman's research produced clear and tangible outcomes: tools and exercises designed to make the city more intelligible to its residents and students. Drawing on architectural skills and studies of perception, with sight privileged as the primary sense, they developed community-generated maps, environmental games, and urban data centers to disseminate information about public space and its uses. De Carlo's work, by contrast, lacks this specificity. His notion of "learning from the city" is broader and more holistic, with little emphasis on the legibility of the city's physical form. It can instead be understood as an immersive engagement with the city's social fabric, an experience that demands interaction with all its actors and the involvement of every sense.

I want to draw attention to the italicization of *experience*, as it is meant to underscore the importance of this concept in De Carlo's understanding of the relationship between pedagogy and space. Halfway through the article, we read:

> Education is the result of experience. The broader and more complex the experience, the deeper and more intense the education. The field of experience widens in direct correlation to the frequency of contacts, and its complexity expands as their variety increases. Ultimately, to ensure a truly profound and stimulating education, no type of experience should be denied: All possible contacts, of whatever nature, should not only be allowed but solicited.[36]

This excerpt highlights De Carlo's rejection of specialization and his pursuit of complexity in architecture, but it also, and foremost, reveals the extent of his ambition. Taking his statement at face value, in fact, would prompt us to realize the impracticality of constructing educational buildings and of the architectural profession as a whole. If we accept that buildings were, even in their scattered form, spatially *delimited* structures, the question arises as to whether they could really be suitable for opening up to *unlimited* experiences, as the sentence suggests. The passage points to an unresolved tension in De Carlo's work between the impossibility of educational containment and the growing need for more physical infrastructure for education in the 1970s,[37] along with the standardized architectural responses that typically addressed such needs.

Before we bring the section to a close and move to the last and final part of this introduction, we must shed some further light on De Carlo's understanding of *experience*, for it offers an antidote to the present *mis*usage of the term in higher education, a term, it must be stressed, that was once fundamental to 1970s radical pedagogy. As we glimpsed in the quotations excerpted, De Carlo sees "experience" as something prominently social and unpredictable, which benefits from the dissolution or, at the very least, disturbance of the enclosed contours of university buildings. Unintentionally echoing John Dewey's definition of the term as shaped by the principles of "continuity" and "interaction," De Carlo advocates for an understanding of experience as constituted through transactions within a community.[38] Seen from this stance, experience transcends the very possibility of individual assessments and exposes the inadequacy of the evaluative procedures in the contemporary university.

* * *

The task of the designer is, first of all, to re-establish with clarity the terms of the class struggle.[39]

Architecture's departure from the physical object was paralleled by the blurring of the line dividing designers and the public, with the word *participation* taking center stage in the discipline. In the mid-1960s, American planner Paul Davidoff and his partner, Linda, conceptualized "advocacy planning," with the aim to challenge the exclusionary logic of post–World War II zoning and open it up to the people.[40] Around the same time, Cedric Price gained notoriety for his "calculated uncertainty," an approach to design that limited the input of architects to the creation of grids, allowing residents to fill them at will. De Carlo also made an important contribution to this new field through both his writing and practice. His 1970s essays "The Public of Architecture" and "An Architecture of Participation"[41] have acquired the status of reference points for generations of architects willing to challenge the traditional top-down approach of the discipline.

In these articles, included in the anthology, De Carlo's idea of participation takes shape against the backdrop of his critique of the modern movement. We should recall, in fact, De Carlo's foundational role in TEAM 10, a group of young architects who withdrew their membership from the Congrès Internationaux d'Architecture Moderne (CIAM) in rebellion against the monolithic predicaments of modernist urbanism. Reflecting on this dissident experience, the texts challenge the rationalizing imperative underpinning the modernist project by offering an unconventional critical reading of one of its highlights: Grete Schütte-Lihotzky's Frankfurt kitchen.

Praised for its use of interviews and motion studies to inform, and seemingly improve, the final design, the Frankfurt kitchen is, for De Carlo, an egregious example of modernism's inability to design for the people as it promised. What designers of the time popularized as the "scientific method" was instead a reversal of the "correct" subject-object relation in design, to the advantage of the latter: "The subject is no longer the person who uses the kitchen but the omelet," as he puts it.[42] His criticism illuminates how the "public" invoked by modernist design as the ultimate recipient was in fact no more than a means, a functioning body that architecture had to put to work in the best way. Distancing himself from this trend, De Carlo seeks to reinstall the users and their agency at the very core of his practice.

He describes this departure as a shift from a "design for" to a "design with" approach, meaning by the latter both the inclusion of future inhabitants at the earliest stages of design and a shared responsibility for a project's outcome (we will return to this later). Yet, in calling for a collaborative relationship between designers and the public, he remains vigilant about idealized conceptions of participation or too generic ideas of what is "public." The stake is not indiscriminately opening the project to future users but more strategically finding ways to include the social demographics *historically excluded* from city planning and siding with them in the class conflict that this inclusion will eventually trigger. De Carlo is aware that the alliance between the designer and future inhabitants is not at all given, as the former are caught up in professional language that is unknown to the latter. How to bridge this gap and allow for participation to take place, then?

The occasion to tackle this problem is offered by the commission for the design of a residential project for the workers of a steel factory in the city of Terni, in central Italy, the famous Matteotti village (1969–1974). Having obtained the approval to involve the future residents by a commissioning board composed of factory CEOs and workers' councils, De Carlo decided to proceed in a rather unconventional manner. In place of resorting to the common sociological tools of direct interviews and questionnaire, he organized an exhibition about residential architectural projects of reputedly high architectural standard and invited all future residents to pay a visit. To better grasp the reason behind this unusual approach, we must momentarily turn to the words of Domenico de Masi, a sociologist involved in the project as a consultant. Recalling the early phases of the work, he states:

> Asking people without experience what type of house and district they desire means obtaining predictable answers: that is, the house of a local doctor in the city of Terni, in other words, the same house as a factory worker, just a bit bigger, with more tiles and a few more options.[43]

As Masi highlights, workers' imagination was shaped by their limited familiarity with architectural typologies as well as by societal pressure associated with class mobility. This rendered the tool of the questionnaire inadequate, for the demands advanced in response to architects' direct questions tended to be modest and of little help for a thorough rethinking of residential spaces. The problem could be addressed only obliquely, first finding ways to awaken workers' imagination and only then inviting them to visualize and articulate their wishes. From these premises emerged the idea of the exhibition. Conceived with a dual purpose, it functioned partly as educational platform, offering workers a panoramic view of high-standard residential projects, and partly as a means of dismantling the one-way relationship between designers and residents, fostering encounters between professional expertise and popular aspirations.

* * *

The concept of the exhibition also highlights the central role of images, and of the imaginative act itself, in De Carlo's understanding of architecture and its transformative potential. In a few places in the texts, De Carlo refers to "realistic utopia," a variant of utopian thinking resting on (imaginative) immersion into the complexity of reality rather than on its eradication. In trying to define this concept, De Carlo writes:

> In its common understanding, utopia presents an impossible image, because it involves a complete alteration of the context to which it is opposed, meaning that it does not take into account

> the variables that constitute reality. If, by contrast, we consider all of these variables and assume that the relations that constitute them could be different—because they could well be—then utopia becomes realistic.[44]

"Utopia" is reframed here as the outcome of a speculative recombination of the real elements at play in socio-urban settings, an exercise that aligns with the multiplication of the viewpoints and solutions offered by the architecture of participation.

De Carlo's unorthodox understanding of the relationship among images, space, and social change chimes with the philosophy of Henri Lefebvre, even if his name never receives much attention.[45] In his monumental *The Production of Space*, Lefebvre advanced the idea of space as social product resulting from the interplay of three elements: the images of the space elaborated from those in power (including planners); the direct, lived experience of space of its inhabitants; and the symbolic values given to places. Within this spatial triad, representations are just as integral to the production of space as the tangible, economic (i.e., structural) dimensions that comprise the built environment.[46] It is precisely here that De Carlo and Lefebvre converge: while maintaining a Marxist reading of architecture and urban planning, both reject rigid distinctions between structure and superstructure, instead proposing a dynamic and reciprocal relationship between the two.

These ideas are articulated by the De Carlo in the following passage from "Architecture's Public":

> Architecture, as a typical superstructural activity, "depends" on the transformation of societal structures. However, it is important to clarify the dialectical terms of this "dependence" to avoid it being oversimplified and used as an alibi for conservatism and abdication.
>
> Structural transformations open up potential space for the renewal of superstructures. But if this renewal is to become reality, it must occur in the superstructures themselves which, in turn, create room for further structural transformations. The new superstructures feed back into the new structural realities, giving their motivations concrete tangibility.[47]

As we read, De Carlo is aware of the economic imbrications of architecture, but he insists on the latter's ability to act back onto the structure, implicitly referring to the possibilities offered by prefigurative devices. Architecture, he states late in the text, has the vantage point of creating images showing "concretely" how the physical environment could look *otherwise*, rousing attention, inspiring, and ultimately triggering transformations of the forces and relations of production adding up to the building industry. The reframing of the relationship between architecture's representations and its structural component also bears an effect on ideas about the designer's political agency, for if we accept that changes can be instigated from the representational realm, designers will have no excuse to "wait in the lair of architecture as-it-exists[,] and hope for a social palingenesis to automatically generate a new kind of architecture."[48]

* * *

The housing scheme exhibition provided the future inhabitants with formal references that could be brought up during a series of conversations, always conducted during working time and without the presence of the bosses. The second stage finally allowed De Carlo and his team to fathom residents' expectations in greater detail and develop five architectural typologies, each composed by three different units, for a total of fifteen variants. Models and plans of the first design proposal were the subject of another exhibition, which allowed the workers to see a mock-up of their houses to be and suggest amendments to their forms. This revision in progress resulted in the introduction of three additional options within each unit, totaling forty-five alternative permutations. In a fourth phase, finally, the team designed ways to join the different parts in a manner that would refrain from imposing a unifying order and respect their discrete character. De Carlo's method transformed composition into a cumulative process of choices, disrupting the grand design traditionally dictated by the architect as demiurge.

The project, however, had a bitter ending. After enthusiasm and warm feedback during the design phase, challenges arose throughout implementation. Firstly, the construction company prevented residents from accessing the building site during construction, citing "technical incompetence" as an excuse. Later, the steel factory decided to change the plan and sell the flats to the residents. The original project had assumed the property would remain in the hands of the factory, along with maintenance costs—a project that seemed to have the agreement of all parties involved. Workers thus became owners before the units were completed, and from that moment onward, De Carlo recalls, began to "talk of raising fences, of sectioning off footpaths to turn them into balconies, of possible upward extension rights."[49]

* * *

While placing "the people" at the heart of his architectural vision, De Carlo never allowed the term to drift into abstraction. He gave it weight, class, and texture—attributes always in motion, as everything is in his kaleidoscopic, ever-shifting mode of thought. *Villaggio Matteotti* stands as a lesson in this regard. Holding fast to the notion of class architecture, the project resists the comfort of myth and the stillness of the ideal. Through this lens, what might first appear a failure becomes a diagnostic flaw awaiting correction in the next round of the combinatory game. This, too, might be seen as an instance of De Carlo's *realistic utopia*.

Luisa Lorenza Corna

The Overturned Pyramid

1.

After the floods and earthquakes, a new cataclysm shakes our country: the revolt of the University.[1]

The strikes; occupations; lockouts; police charges; the suspended, imprisoned, wounded students; the disbarred professors; the confused deans; the bewildered ministers; all the ineptitude and violence that were unexpectedly revealed, cast a bad conscience that not even the *chains of solidarity* could exorcise.

For a conformist country with an authoritarian structure like ours, the revolt of the University is as inconceivable as the rebellion of the military academies, of the police or the prisoners. If the University is in revolt, the whole structure of the nation falters: it is cause for both scandal and despair. In fact, the University, like the military academies, is considered a crucible for operators whose role is to make the system work. In the name of preserving and safeguarding the system, professors and students, like police and prisoners, are, respectively, the initiators and disciples, the redeemers and redeemed of the system.

If the University is in revolt, the established social order loses any guarantee of future continuation. What is more, and this is worse, it risks throwing into confusion its fundamental values. Clear distinctions, predetermined by the established order, between good and evil, right and wrong, efficiency and waste, and so on, end up being dissolved in a disturbing and dangerous sequence of dialectical nuances.

In Italy, the term "university" promptly conjures up the rhetorical image of the medieval University: a total community of teachers and students linked by common interest in and responsibility for research, embedded into a fair federation of free Communes; a societal structure that is anchored in the present reality and projected toward a future utopia.

But the medieval image that, in our country, is usually attached to the idea of the University is hopelessly rhetorical. Since the Middle Ages, our University has undergone such radical transformations that it has completely lost its original connotations. The contemporary Italian University bears instead the later imprint of the Society of Jesuits and the unification of the Italian State. That authoritarian and instrumental conformation was to be further confirmed by subsequent historical events and is today the main cause of its backwardness and troubles.

With the Jesuits at the end of the sixteenth century, the principle of authority entered the Italian University, as well as the Universities of the Catholic area, and along with it came the germ that corroded the free movement of ideas which had characterized the communities of study during the Middle Ages. Culture was placed at the service of an indisputable and superior reason, which imposed the erection of a disciplinary and hierarchical apparatus. The idea of independent research, articulated according to the needs of its own rationality, became suspect in the context of an ideological fundamentalism that demanded orthodoxy and conformism.

When we rightly celebrate the glory of our Universities in the period of the Counter-Reformation, we should always specify that such glory is due to a few groups of scholars who continued to challenge the system by pursing universal research which went against the official tendency of the institutions they were part of. In opposition to outliers like Galileo stood Mr. Priuli and Lodovico delle Colombe, who represented the large majority and were in effect the Real University. The Real University was in fact a rigid institution, controlled by fundamentalists and governed by Aristotelians. It went through a continuous series of involutions before reaching that condition of provincial obtusity and clientelism in which the Royal Commissioners found it around 1860, when the unified Italian State began to address the problems of reunification and how to relaunch higher education. In those years the newly formed Italian State took into consideration the German and French models. In keeping with the characteristic obtusity of its common sense, it managed to capture the worst of both. From the German model it took the vocation to detach itself from the global needs of society, in the name of an idealistic preservation of the harmony of knowledge. It neglected instead the principle of bold and independent exchange that was at the basis of Wilhelm von Humboldt's program for the foundation of Higher Scientific Institutions in Berlin.[2] From the French model it disregarded its pragmatic content to embrace instead the authoritarian agendas of the University as a *state monopoly*.

The real intentions of the various ministers in charge of education in Italy from 1859 to the present day—from Gabrio Casati onward (with the exception of Francesco De Sanctis and, in a different sense, Giovanni Gentile)—rather than by the flood of words they pronounced, are far better represented by the blunt statements that Napoleon I delivered to the Council of State on March 21, 1810: "If my hopes are fulfilled, I want to find in the Academic Body a safeguard against pernicious theories that tend to subvert the established social order. . . . The Academic Body will have the task of first sounding the alarm and then be ready to resist the dangerous theories of those singular spirits . . . who seek to stir public opinion."[3] These intentions, counterbalanced by a sequence of calculated calls for a culture uncontaminated by politics, constitute the ideological framework on which the Italian University has so far been based. The state-monopoly University represented the most appropriate instrument for the bourgeoisie as the state-monopolizing class. But with the transition from an entirely agricultural to a partially industrial economy, and with the strengthening and proliferation of the state bureaucracy, the bourgeoisie was gripped by a new set of demands that forced it to readjust its apparatus of public education.

As an instrument of ideological control and preservation of power, the University was now expected to fulfill the urgent task of providing executives for the management of both the state and its new productive structures. At this point, the initial objective of the University appeared under a new light: It became a question of combining new contingent needs with its core authoritarian requirement. To achieve this, it was necessary to maximize the instrumentalization of the executives produced. In other words, their training had to be oriented toward purely operational and sectoral ends, destroying any germ of free research and criticism within an organizational system that would automatically engender the reasons for its agnosticism. After the objectives and strategy to achieve them had been established, fascism further fine-tuned this operation, using for its purposes both the wisdom and ignorance, the subtleties and obtusity of the class it served.

The Reform named after Giovanni Gentile consisted of two stages, which accurately represent the deep-rooted habit of the Italian bourgeoisie to boast about its love for chastity at the very moment of its prostitution. The first stage corresponds to the delineation of an idealistic framework which revives, in Fichtian terms, the idea of culture as detached from the horrible contingencies of reality so as not to be tainted by vulgarity and oppression. The second occurs when vulgarity and oppression invade the picture and impose their own rules, without encountering any cultural resistance beyond a heartfelt (and smug) regret.[4]

When in 1923 he approved the Gentile Reform, Mussolini was already aware of the radical revisions he would soon make to it so that it better served his ends. He expressed his thoughts in unequivocal terms: "The fascist government needs a ruling class. In the experience of the past fourteen months of government, I realized that this ruling class does not exist. I cannot rustle up improvised functionaries across the entire administration: these should be provided to me rank by rank by the University. . . . The fascists have a duty to act so that the Universities will produce a ruling class properly qualified for its great and difficult duties." What measures were taken to implement such a program? What were the rules imposed on the University by vulgarity and oppression? The same rules that govern the structure of the Italian University today, after the war, the resistance, and twenty years of parliamentary debate. The same rules that we would have had tomorrow if the new Reform had been approved at the Chamber of Deputies—that is, if the students' revolt had not succeeded in overturning the terms of the problem.[5] Today, as at the time of the Jesuits, these rules are based on the principle of authority, yet there is a perceptible and significant difference. This principle, source of the most serious evils that afflicted and continue to afflict the world, had, in Ignatius of Loyola's conception, a transcendent and universal character, and an irreducible and hard rigor, however cruel it might have been. Instead, the principle of authority on which the structure of the modern-day University stands has turned into a quagmire of compromise and corruption, where any possibility of contradiction and thus redemption drowns.

From the application of the principle of authority, the University derives its organization in sealed-off compartments, necessarily and permanently opposed to each other. The first fundamental barrier is between lecturers and students. Lecturers are those who know, and students are those who do not know. But what do these opposite sides know or not know? Naturally they possess or do not possess knowledge; but that is not all. Besides knowledge, students do not know the reasons why they should know, nor the ways in which such reasons are governed. They do not and are not supposed to know the structure and forms of these modes of governance. They do not participate, discuss nor decide, but are accidental and extraneous passengers of an institution that should be made for them and whose only reason to exist is their presence.

Another series of barriers hermetically divides the lecturers. There are voluntary assistants, tenured assistants, adjuncts, visiting professors, tenured professors, institute directors, deans, rectors. Here the barriers are horizontal, and their stratifications give rise to a pyramid whose edges vanish at the top into a dark band. An external observer judging their convergence might imagine the pyramid's apex to be close and concrete; but, in reality, the apex is not there. Beyond the dark and indecipherable band, the edges diverge and, shooting off in different directions, enter the tangled structure of the State. It is here, where the most unpredictable convergences and plots take place, that the University finds its most covert and indissoluble links with the system.

After all, apart from voluntary assistants and adjunct professors—spermatozoa feverishly in search of an egg that will give them concrete configuration—all other lecturers, at different levels of the pyramid, are civil servants. The walls that divide them into hierarchical categories are upwardly permeable: Everyone can move up, even if their chances are low. But what regulates this ascent is not, as one would like to believe, scientific value; the rise is rather the product of a complicated and cruel rite of initiation whose final outcome is the acceptance of or forced connivance with the system. The climbing passes through a succession of steps perfectly calibrated to filter out independence, the courage to state one's opinion, as well as scientific and human loyalty. Those who made it to the top—even when, by chance or thanks to natural resolve, they managed to retain some dignity and decorum—all carry engraved in the innermost layers of their personal history the shame of having submitted to a temporary or definitive capitulation. The rules of the game are perfect because, like in *The Glass Bead Game* or in poker, the cycle never comes to an end: No one can ever consider themselves on top, for the simple reason that the top is not there. The motivation for playing the game is also perfect, since its logic is based on *achieving power*. Each stage achieved comes with new inalienable privileges and prizes, which are designated by power and are absolute in themselves.[6]

To give an example that in different terms applies to each level attained: A tenured professor cannot be dismissed from his position even if due to premature senility he is no longer able to teach; nor even if for selfish, private interests he neglects or refuses to teach, employs assistants and students as labor-power for his personal extracurricular initiatives, or uses his university rank to increase his prestige and earnings in the professional field. Whether senile or committed, profiteering or disinterested, in any case he has the absolute prerogative of setting and maneuvering the filters that protect his position from the penetration of the lower ranks. In circumstances of supreme defense (and maximum corruption), the automatic response of the system is for everyone to close ranks; all, even against their personal convictions, are automatically drawn into a whirlpool of abstract manipulations (and shameful alliances).

Through these automatic processes, which transcend and at the same time involve the will of individuals, the University presents itself as a center of power that has nothing to do with the demands of teaching and culture. It becomes one subset within the more general set of centers of power that are located within the State or that govern it from the outside.[7]

For those who are still incredulous or simply too fond of the rhetorical myth of the pristine and ineffable University, we could point to many situations and countless data. But no detailed account could be more persuasive than the indisputable fact that the Rectors, with the consent of the Faculty Boards, have in recent years repeatedly called in the police to clear the Universities from protesting students.

For centuries, the right to freely contest the system was recognized and enshrined by the autonomy of the academic community. The appeal to that system for the restoration of an authoritarian order by violent means constitutes, on the one hand, an explicit demonstration of the abuse inflicted on the communitarian balance. On the other hand, it reveals the links of the abusing party with the external forces of the establishment. The establishment needs executives, but it wants to obtain them from a University that acquiesces to its demands. Moreover, the answers to its demands do not necessarily need to come through the University. If it were possible to create new institutions already instrumentalized from the start, these would provide greater guarantees than a controlled but restless University, which, at least in some of its parts, shows sympathy with the call of protest. The plan to divide higher education into, on the one hand, an educational sector for the preparation of operational executives through the courses offered by a downgraded (and decentralized) University and, on the other, a research sector entrusted to industrial monopolies, and hence endowed with plenty of technical instruments and economic means, is neither new nor far-fetched. More imaginative observers might wonder whether this is not precisely the plan that in recent years the State has been pursuing in its, as yet far too brief, journey toward finding a solution to the problem of the mass University. These observers might even wonder whether the definition of *tiers*, in the imprecise and ambiguous meaning given to them by the new proposed bill, does not in effect preclude, however confusingly, precisely the realization of that idea: For the Gui plan, despite all its Morotean softness,[8] tends toward the same instrumentalizing intentions as the Gaullist Fouchet plan.[9]

After all, it was the suspicion provoked by such plan that a few years ago sparked the student revolt which today so deeply anguishes the nation.

The initial demands of the students were directed to the quantitative aspects of the problem. The main topics raised by the students in the first stage of the debate around 1960 were in fact: inefficient territorial distribution of the universities; inadequate campuses; lack of classrooms and workspaces; insufficient educational resources; nonexistent student accommodations and cultural, sports, health, and welfare facilities; and, above all, delays in issuing scholarships and grants considered a fundamental means to concretely implement the right to education set forth by the Constitution.

Interestingly, at this stage the students' theories tended to coincide with the views and programs of the official left-wing parties. For both, quite reasonably, the solution to quantitative problems was a matter for the State; indeed, it was only possible after having implemented a rigorous concentration of all instruments of education in state-run organizations, radically cutting off any possibility of initiatives outside the state.

Even more interesting, however, is to note how the second, qualitative phase, which has developed in recent months, has moved beyond the resolute oversimplification of this assumption. While some sectors of the parliamentary left continue to assure their unconditional support for the university struggles, many student groups, who have achieved a greater degree of articulation through a progressive refinement of their theories, have started to wonder whether the left-wing parties, instead of fighting for a generalized statism, would not have done better to promote radical alternatives to the existing structures. They wonder whether their actions, despite the undeniable cosmetic reforms they brought, did not ultimately contribute to confirm and strengthen the system.

This question signals a burning issue requiring an evaluation of both the parliamentary left's real points of contestation and the ultimate meaning of a youth revolt that has recently exploded *everywhere*, not just in the University and not just in Italy. This is a twofold problem consisting, on the one hand, in the aging of traditional political structures and, on the other, in the emergence of new modes of political action. These new modes of action place themselves outside the conventional struggles for political power which are rejected in favor of a tension of absolute and irreducible protest.[10]

On this occasion, I can only offer a cursory sketch of the transition from the quantitative to the qualitative phase, from a rationalizing attitude to an action of total contestation calling into question the very rationale that holds the system together. In any case this transition is best illustrated by a few fragments taken from the document that the students of Turin produced during the last occupation of Palazzo Campana:

> "The University of today does not respond to the needs posed by the demand for labor arising from society. Our objective, however, is not merely to adapt it to the needs of such a labor demand. We believe that the University must and can provide those who attend it with both . . . adequate professional preparation and tools for criticism"; "We are victims of a despotic system that disaccustoms us to political discussion and struggle while imposing its authoritarian and subordinating politics on us"; "Professors should not be our masters, but should participate in seminars and research on equal footing, putting their expertise at the service of study groups "; "The students—future industry managers, civil servants, or teachers—are no longer able to set up a political discussion with their peers. They thought they were going to university to learn history, law, physics, medicine; instead, they have learned above all to command and obey."

If we coolly examine these plain statements, we cannot help but recognize that they contain far more imaginative novelty and foresight than what can be detected in the proposals and threats of their failed masters. Following the trajectory of a long revolt, students have arrived on their own at the crux of the problem. They now propose a new "definition" of the Italian University and, beyond that, a new "definition" of society.[11]

2.

In the recent history of university revolts, the Faculties of Architecture have played a particularly prominent role. I will try to outline the main aspects of this role through a series of brief observations.

First of All, Briefly, the Facts

In December 1963, shortly after the start of the academic year, the students of architectural composition at the Faculty of Architecture in Milan went on strike. A few weeks earlier, considering the topics of their assignments outdated and abstract, they had asked lecturers for a free debate on the contents of the program. Faced with refusal, they proclaimed a strike and after an alternating series of promises and threats, together with the students of all the other courses, they occupied the faculty building in February 1964. It was the first time that students had occupied an Italian Faculty and the first sensational episode of university revolt.[12]

A few months later, the example of Milan was taken up by the architectural faculties of Turin and Rome, where similar situations and identical behaviors led the students first to a series of strikes and then to an occupation. Barricaded in their quarters, the students began to examine their problems together. Before long, the initial incidents proved to be negligible compared to the underlying issues that started surfacing: clarification of the tasks that the architect is called on to perform in society; definition of the type of preparation that the Faculty should provide to ensure the performance of these tasks in society; modification of the Faculty's structure so as to make it suitable for providing the architect with the necessary type of preparation; demolition of the compartmentalization of programs; transformation of Institutes into bodies intended to promote research; renewal of faculty members so that they better correspond to its new orientation; co-participation of students in decision-making processes related to the cultural management of the school.

Among all these issues—related and made inseparable by an internal logic—the most astute Faculty Boards singled out only the last two. The most ill-advised, instead, rejected them entirely, planning to resolve the crisis through an intensification of disciplinary rigor. To appease the students' desire for participation, Joint Commissions were invented. To plug the holes resulting from a long period of isolation and cultural involution, a number of new professors were recruited from other Universities or were brought into the academic ranks from the professional world. For some time, both expedients proved effective. Indeed, during 1965 and part of 1966, while the revolt was spreading to all the other Faculties, in the Faculty of Architecture, the tensions faded into a futile situation of waiting for internal renewal and the wearisome skirmishes of bureaucratic disputes. The *new* professors were seen as such mainly because they represented more modern professional or critical tendencies than those advocated by the academic staff who had hitherto dominated the school. The latter's dominance of the most important power centers of the universities had been so total that their obscurantist selections had determined the entire spectrum of architectural activity. To be admitted to the school, had one to demonstrate not only absolute backwardness in general conceptions but also backwardness in professional and critical choices. Thus, by inference, at least the students started thinking that those individuals whose productions were new would also produce *new* scholarly research. They failed to consider that beyond the very narrow limits of an individual's behavior, there need not be a coherent correspondence between activities and general conceptions; or else the latter might be only indirect and implicit, making it impossible to transform them into general action. Above all, they did not consider that isolated individuals count for little in relation to structures—and all the less the more heinous and corrupting those structures are. Even the new professors allowed themselves to be taken in by the system's game; instead of subverting the rules, they simply played by them—mostly, but not always—with greater decorum. The same amount of time and disappointment led to the unravelling of the real function of the Joint Commissions.

Joint Commissions were generally comprised of the Rector or Dean, three tenured professors, three adjunct professors, three assistants, and three students. Their task was to give advisory opinions to the Faculty Boards on problems of cultural management. But members of the Faculty Boards—namely the Rector and the tenured professors—were also present in the Commission, while retaining, however, the prerogative of taking the final decision. Before long, the students, and later the assistants and adjuncts, realized that under no circumstances can parity be implemented between groups that hold all the authority and power and groups that have none. The issues discussed in the Joint Commissions were invariably marginal and, in any case, even the few conclusions painstakingly reached were refuted or tweaked when they were passed on to the decision-making bodies: the Faculty Board or the Board of Trustees or even, when necessary, the Higher Council of the Ministry of Education. The students also came to another, far more serious and dangerous realization: that their representatives in the Joint Commission were themselves caught up, or more literally wrapped up, in the logic of the system they were supposed to oppose and ended up losing their ties with the Student Assembly, the real source of their innovative energy.

After this period of experiences and unmet expectations, the fundamental problems that had been temporarily shelved returned to the center of the debate. It was clear that all the issues that came into focus during the 1963 occupations could not be addressed and resolved other than through a profound and simultaneous reform of the contents and structures of the Faculty. In 1967, taking once again its cue from a series of protests aimed at the most defective and antiquated teaching sectors, the struggle was rekindled and later turned into a global action against the power of the Faculty Boards.

In Milan, Turin, Naples, and Venice, students occupied the Faculties of Architecture. All occupations, except in Milan, were cleared by the police. In Venice, where the occupation had been longer and more resolute than elsewhere, it was not the Rector who called for police intervention, but a neo-fascist movement that went under the name of Ordine Nuovo (New Order), even though it was actually devoted to the preservation of the old order, wherever it could still be found and, hence, especially in the University.

These, in brief, are the facts. The second observations refer to

The Opposing Parties and Their Current Relations

At the beginning of the new academic year, the Faculties of Architecture seemed relatively quiet. Only recently, prompted by broader external events, has the unrest resumed with vigor, in several cases resulting in the occupation of university campuses. However, even in occupied Faculties, seminars continue to be held where, with the participation of lecturers, work programs for the coming months are discussed or finalized. The internal situation, which appears to have calmed down, is actually suspended in an unstable state of balance, comprising innumerable tensions. In fact, none of the problems that arose during the hottest period of the crisis have been resolved: The preexisting structure is intact and the principle of authority that organizes it has not suffered any noticeable cracks. The only noticeable changes can be found in the behavior of the various parties and especially in the tactics that the most senior parties are developing for the new circumstances, with as little strategic alterations as possible.

For the Faculty Boards this is the time of the *doves*, while for the subordinate and precarious categories of the adjuncts and the assistants, it is the time of the *hawks*. Alliances arise, by spontaneous attraction, between those who wield all the power and those who want to get hold of it as soon as possible: Both sides find in the other the promise of mutual support.

In some cases, the Faculty Boards govern prudently; in others, they don't govern at all and leave the initiative to the students to propose new forms of school organization for a forthcoming period of activity which everyone agrees to consider experimental. The outcome of this initiative is likely to be twofold: it might bring new ideas for a technical reform of the teaching and research sectors; or it may bring no ideas at all, ultimately revealing a confusion of ideas. In the first scenario, results can be achieved through subsequent negotiations; the second scenario can instead be used to incontrovertibly prove that when there is no principle of authority, disorder and powerlessness ensue.

The doves of the Faculty Boards with all sincerity expect the first eventuality; the hawks, with equal sincerity, anticipate the second. But the real issue has nothing to do with the probability of either eventuality taking place. The real issue is that even if the most positive of the two possibilities came to pass, the fundamental structure of the institution would remain unchanged. The operation allowed by the Faculty Boards in this new phase of the crisis has a predominantly instrumental function and as such, once again, it compels political and ideological estrangement.

As for the other categories of lecturers—the adjuncts and the assistants—besides the alliances struck on a personal level, they went back to an almost irrelevant position. The leading role that the assistants had taken alongside the students and adjuncts against the tenured during the most heated period of the previous occupations is now a distant memory.[13] Students are the only real interlocutors of the Faculty Boards left.

It should go without saying that students are not a social class—and this is true, of course, of the entire University, not just the Faculty of Architecture. Nonetheless, this image has been widely exploited, by supporters and external opponents alike, to establish sociological analogies and draw political interpretations. Even if part of the students' demands has an economic basis—concrete accessibility to higher education for all social classes, comprehensive grants, housing and employment rights, and so on—the condition of university students is that of an heterogenous group destined for specific social functions. The real problem for students is not so much that of acquiring economic security, but rather of clarifying the objectives of their role, the reasons why they should assume it, and the ways in which they can carry it out. The prerequisite for this process of clarification is that it comes from the students themselves, because only then will they have the guarantee that the objectives will not be inhuman, that the reasons will not be overpowering, and that the methods will not be agnostic. In other words, only then will this clarification serve as a guarantee that they will not be instrumentalized in the exercise of the social role for which they are training; that their lives will have human meaning.

The question therefore arises for the students in terms of "emancipation" and is part of the broader phenomenon of the expansion of civil rights. On this new frontier, the youth is on the move all around the world, from the United States to Europe and China, to gain an autonomy of expression that has always been denied in the name of the long-standing and trans-classist affirmation of the principle of authority: the uncontested dominance of older generations in the government of society. From different standpoints, appropriate to the different ideological and political conditions of each country, the movement has converged toward an identical goal: the affirmation of the right of young people to challenge the actions of a society that fails disastrously on a human level at the very moment in which it has reached the peak of productive efficiency.

This growing awareness, the same that presently grips university students, has profound analogies with the revolts of colonized people and of Afro-Americans associated with Black Power. It passes through an initial phase of self-definition and then, in a later phase, manifests original forms of expression and struggle that radically repudiate the rationality of the system and totally refuse even the most advanced structures produced by it.[14]

In the course of their struggle against the Faculty Boards, the students of the Faculties of Architecture have sought, perhaps earlier than others, organizational forms and modes of conduc,t which, precisely because of their novelty, have proved to be concretely subversive. While in the first half of the revolt the traditional student associations representing political tendencies that mirrored those of the institutional parties played a fundamental role, they now tend to assume a predominantly marginal organizational function. The All-Students' Assembly has become the sovereign body. Delegations of representatives are kept to a minimum: In many Faculties, the president of the Assembly and delegates liaising with lecturers or external bodies are replaced daily. This causes delays and some confusion, but at the same time it averts the risk of power crystallizing, while generating participation, awareness, and hence freedom (and the students are convinced that, contrary to what they have been taught, freedom matters more than efficiency). In one of the Faculties of Architecture during the occupation, students had organized themselves into independent groupings, very similar to Jacobin clubs, corresponding to different tendencies of opinion. It was considered neither shameful nor disgraceful to switch from one group to another if one happened to change one's opinion during the development of the debate. In another Faculty of Architecture, students dug up a courtyard, where professors used to park their cars, to transform it into a garden. Some might think that these two cases are too different in kind to compare, and yet, in essence, they are part of the same struggle. However, amid these and many other new forms of conduct that grew out of the unrest of the occupation, there are still uncertainties springing from the horror of an institutional vacuum and the nostalgia for reassuring apparatuses. Especially in the ranks of official student representatives, there is no shortage of "Uncle Toms" concerned with putting a stop to the operation as soon as possible to balance the faculty's accounts in such a way as to include their admittedly precarious function.

During recent planning seminars, managers, already emboldened by their academic power, attempted several times to reconcile disagreements on the fragile basis of the first results achieved. In contrast, while the Assembly was sometimes distracted by matters of detail, it was always present and adamant on matters of principle.

Thus, Faculty Boards and Student Assemblies, with their opposing attitudes, are the only parties that currently count in the Italian Faculties of Architecture. As in all the other Faculties, the key fault line that divides the two parties can be traced back to the principle of authority. The question is to understand what material factors underlie this line. The third observation is therefore about

The Faculty as a Place of Crisis

The foundations of the crisis in the Faculty of Architecture are obviously related to the more general crisis of the Italian University, but they also derive from its specific formation and the cultural context of which it is part. There are seven schools of Architecture in Italy: in Turin, Milan, Venice, Florence, Rome, Naples, and Palermo (plus half a school in Genoa, limited to a two-year foundational course). All of them, except that of Genoa, became universities from 1925 to 1935, through a series of similar transformations, and took as their main models the courses of *architectural drawing* in the Academies of Fine Arts and those of *civic architecture* in the Polytechnic. The new Faculty of Architecture was born by grafting these two withered branches together, yet it could not find the energy needed to resolve the contradiction between art and technique on which it had been founded. On the contrary, it soon became the place where this contradiction was pushed to the extreme, becoming an exemplary case of a more general disagreement, typical of the Italian cultural milieu, between humanistic and scientific culture. After all, the solutions put forward in the original curricula relied on the naïve expedient of achieving a synthesis through the coexistence of different subjects borrowed from the two opposing fields: the mathematical and technical teachings of construction engineering alongside the historical and decorative teachings of the academies. The hope was for the integration to emerge independently through some concluding modules focused on so-called architectural composition.

But this integration did not take place. Depending on the weight given to one field or the other, the new Faculty was in its various incarnations either more *academic* or more *technical*. In no instance was it a *school of architecture* according to the precise meaning that architectural activity was acquiring in actual practice.

Later, as this meaning continued expanding, new subjects were added to preexisting ones, making curricula even more inefficient and the school's activities increasingly impracticable. Without a goal to aim toward and incapable of disentangling the elements of a cultural tendency from its institutional confusion, the Faculty failed to carry out either abstract or applied research. It limited itself to the mere exercise of a didactic approach that would remain bureaucratic in scientific subjects, conventional in artistic subjects and non-systematic in compositional subjects. In relation to this way of conceiving of the school and education, teaching staff were selected from professional settings or academic mausoleums. These were often established, and hence already old, personalities who were incapable of finding in the university any other reason for commitment beyond the strengthening of their personal position.

Anything good achieved in Italian architecture has very rarely come from the universities. If we were to look for the authors of such "good things," we would realize that often they were either self-taught, or came from other Faculties, or had received their education elsewhere: in the most qualified professional studios, in the editorial offices of magazines, in books that were hardly ever written by their professors. Very few of these survivors were able to return to the university to bring back, as lecturers, the experience of what they had learned elsewhere. Giuseppe Pagano did not return, despite the stimulating influence he exerted on young people from the outside. Nor did Irenio Diotallevi or Franco Marescotti, even though they were the only ones who conducted serious research in Italian architecture in the period between the two wars. Some, like Ernesto Rogers, among the very few who were able to return to the university after the 1950s, were forced to stay at the gallows while antidotes were prepared to neutralize their influence. First with exclusions and later with a calculated dose of discrimination and neutralization, the Faculty of Architecture was able to keep its original flaws intact. Today, as at the time of its founding, an intricate tangle of contradictory components obscures its ends, blurs its tensions, and cancels out its competences. It has repercussions on the ongoing debate, often making it impossible to clarify its ultimate consequences. In the more general context of current university attitudes, this hesitation seems typical of the Faculties of Architecture, so it feels appropriate to elucidate its reasons by focusing the fourth observation on

The Terms of the Debate

In 1930, during the inauguration of the Faculty of Architecture in Florence, the academic luminary Ugo Ojetti established a set of parameters intended to guide the conduct of professors and students.

"The School of Architecture," he said, "must be the school where hierarchies are taught and respected." By this he meant the hierarchy of buildings that opposes monuments to the "factories for all," but he also meant the hierarchy "that is in men and in society." He welded the two poles of his thesis into the negative image of reinforced concrete which is "composed of two contradictory elements, that is iron and liquid slime." This image was offered as a symbol of a precarious civilization, "fortunately not Italian, which strives to direct the fleeting, mutable, and liquid crowd around the more or less pliable iron of authority." The anchorage in tradition would have averted both the use of such "composite" technologies and the introduction of the "leveling" ideologies they implied.

Later, from the same platform, the Honorable Professor Alberto Calza Bini tried to skirt around the political difficulties of the time with an invitation "to narrate for posterity through artistic form the power and faith of Mussolini's Italy," thus establishing the opposite direction for the school's tendencies. "Not only the monuments," he said, "but all the built expressions of the new cities . . . must be . . . worthy of the present historical era." Therefore, students should be trained to conceive buildings not only "by virtue of a lyrical sensibility," but also "through the distributive and functional study of the various elements, to gradually arrive at the final architectural expression."

In the oscillating field of these two opposing tensions, the school of architecture continued to define and redefine itself by offsetting the alternating prevalence of one over the other with the creation of an immense range of subjects in permanent contradiction. From the outside, Giuseppe Pagano tried in vain to propose reshaping the entire pedagogical structure by radically demystifying the aims of architecture. Instead, students went on studying the octagonal layouts of factories, the double sapwood of timbers, the structure of the Syriac Basilica, the innumerable and incoherent molecular multitudes, the floor leveling of plazas, the detailed study of doors, the architecture of fountains and water, the manufacture of iron and steel, and so forth. Summing up his schooling, a graduating student put it like this: “The result is that the architect becomes a mathematician, a physicist, a building engineer, an art historian . . . and in any case, he remains an amateur.”

In the years immediately after the Second World War, a debate arose around these grotesque shortcomings of the architect’s training. The first timid demands made by students were in fact aimed at the downsizing of scientific subjects. On that occasion, in the slightly more advanced schools where a minimum dialogue with the lecturers of the so-called artistic subjects was allowed, the first mistakes were made. With the good intention of lightening the syllabus, the level of mathematics and science was reduced, consequently making these subjects instrumental to the apparatus of compositional subjects, that remained as sclerotic and nonsensical as before. The problem could not be solved by simply pruning the branches but required dismantling the trunk and rejuvenating the roots. Indeed, already in 1959, at a lecturers' convention held in Naples, students tabled a motion that pushed the goal forward. "The adjustment of the curriculum," it read, "implies an increase in sensitivity towards the demands of external reality, that is, the problems and needs of the country." Although not explicitly stated at that convention, where students were still paternalistically welcomed as spectators, the question of the country and the urgency of its needs came to the surface, taking the form of a new commitment for architectural activity toward the development of society.

In the following years, the discussion, which was driven by the students' growing discontent and by a series of objective facts that began to emerge from the outside, orbited around these issues. The economic development of the early 1960s had dazzlingly revealed how unprepared Italian architecture was to deal with the phenomena that were being unleashed. The great transformations of the physical environment caused by internal migration, urbanization, increased mobility, and rising incomes, were left to the piracy of private speculators, the abuse of monopolies, and the unreliability of politicians. Not only did architectural training fail to provide executives capable of carrying out correctly the operations with which they were tasked, but it also failed to provide ideas, conceptions, and proposals that could challenge a general lack of culture. The school of architecture continued churning out an elite of generic professionals destined only to satisfy the decorative superfluities of a wealthy elite. However, it had not created operators for territorial planning, nor urbanists nor authentic designers; even less had it produced a culture premised on a systemic and sustained practice of research.[15]

During the strikes and occupations of 1962 and 1963, the students started thinking about this unfortunate situation and the fate in store for them when they left school, with no skills or recognizable part to play in an indecipherable world. The conclusions, put in the very concrete terms of self-defense, set out three main topics: the establishment of a mass Faculty, a renewal of teaching, and the launch of new research activities. These topics were proposed to the professors, inviting them to participate in a common effort of clarification and reorganization. If today, from the deepest point of the crisis, we reexamine the documents which contained that invitation, peremptory in form but open in substance, it appears unclear why the Faculty Boards refused to accept them, playing with reticence and digression, or even laying out the reasons why they considered them an affront to their professional dignity. Undoubtedly, the old authoritarian vice and the obtuse and patronizing cunning typical of the Italian University were at work. But more was at stake in the Faculty of Architecture.

The problem of the mass Faculty corresponded to that of an architecture for the Great Number: The student population has grown because the social demand for architects is objectively expanding and, in turn, Italian architecture has (tendentially) evolved from the decorative superfluity it used to be into a structural necessity for the country's development. But how many of the professors who clung to the safe rock of their academic posts were ready to take on the risk of this new prospect? How many of those who were trained in the province of good taste, of petty professional maneuvers and wishful declamations could take on a commitment to social responsibility?

Moreover, educational renewal corresponded to the formation of a scientific basis for an architecture of the Great Number. The control of the major transformations of the human habitat and the almost unlimited production of objects placed in the physical environment, necessitated the adoption of precise instruments of analysis and planning intervention, based on complex and rigorous techniques. For this reason, to replace furnishing and decoration, design was born out of the school as a complementary activity to the production of everything; and for the same reason, to replace urban architecture after a long period of community tinkering, urban planning started emerging out of the school as a social science. But how many of the professors, who are now ingrained in the professional-artistic pastiche of the school, would be willing to reflect on their cultural background by comparing it with a truly scientific didactic apparatus? Since they had accepted the downgrading of mathematics and science as a way of hiding their inconsistency, they would have never consented to their reintroduction at the maximum level required. Neither would they have allowed for the initiation of genuine research activities, since in a precarious country like ours and in an uncertain field like that of Italian architecture, research corresponds to radical contestation.

For what do those who carry out research discover in the modes through which the physical structures of our country are being shaped? They find that these modes are conditioned by the peculiar needs of an idiotic and oppressive system; that the architectural interventions these modes consist of, even when camouflaged as refined sophistication, function within such a system to enrich it with idiocy and oppression. The activity of research could only be accepted insofar as it was not authentic; that is, insofar as it elicited consent even while presenting itself as contentious; or, on the other hand, insofar as it was able, by mystifying itself, to reabsorb in one fell swoop its own subversive tensions alongside those implied by the mass Faculty and the development of a new didactics.

The Faculty Boards and the most astute members of the subordinate teaching strata were prepared to use this diversionary tactic to stall any changes. The aim of substantially recomposing the old balance of powers justified the use of any formal means, including the liquidation of some adulterated superstructural elements that had become uncomfortable for everyone.

The last stages of the debate have culminated in this ambiguous situation. The danger that everything may remain at a standstill, in a state of simulated accord, prompts us to expand on the subject a little further with a fifth observation referring to

The Example of a Dead-End Solution

At the beginning of the current academic year, architecture students in Milan, having concluded that the Faculty Board was unable to meet their expectations, declared it *effectively defunct* and took on the task of formulating the academic programs themselves. The initial aims were twofold: first, to eliminate the division in courses, which resulted in the obligation of the fixed curriculum; and second, to turn all teaching into research so as to solve the pedagogical problem deriving from the requirements of the mass Faculty.

The first aim was indisputable. If students are unable to choose among the multiple directions that architecture branches off into, and have to pursue them all, thus accumulating repetitive and conflicting notions, they are not just exerting themselves unnecessarily but will ultimately achieve a superficial and inconsistent training. After all, the free definition of one's curriculum within a framework that guarantees every possible outlet is the foundation of a modern and democratic University where the autonomy of teaching equals the autonomy of learning.

In contrast, the second aim was confusing. The confusion was primarily cultural and related to the meaning being ascribed to research. This is hardly surprising given that the material handled in the Faculties of Architecture is so heterogenous and mystified as to obscure any possible interpretation: In an environment where efforts at systematization are seen as curbing the imagination, research could only be undertaken as an exorcising expedient. Secondly, this confusion was political, for the students, in taking on the task of organizing the programs, moved into the lecturers' territory and relieved them of the responsibilities to which they should have continued to commit themselves.

The students requested of all faculty members who had been raised to the rank of researchers, whatever their academic title, and a few experts brought in as collaborators from outside, to present possible research programs that they themselves would have later selected and arranged to configure a new pedagogical structure. Apart from the lecturers of scientific subjects (who, shocked by both the novelty and imprecision of the request, behaved in a way that was consistent with their usual stance of agnostic arrogance), everyone else answered the call and put forward a wide variety of proposals: a sea of platitudes and vague ramblings in which there floated some rigorous and stimulating fragments. All sorts of things were proposed: from explorations in *urbantecture* to the definition of simple *cognitive models*; from the invention of *formal technologies* to traffic-detection systems; from the classification of library books to the execution of personal works *on behalf of third parties* for which commissions were secured.

This panorama alone was more than enough to reveal the shortcomings of the existing academic body and to motivate a further push toward the demolition of their unjustified privileges. Yet the students, embroiled in the program that they themselves had initiated, began the task of selection and sorting. After a long series of debates, they settled on a scheme in which the various research paths, considered either formative or instrumental, particular or professional, were intertwined and pitted against each other with the usual confusion of contents and trends.

This new pastiche of research was mostly due to the poor cultural quality that characterized much of the material received, but it was also due to another fact, far more relevant to the broader issue of the renewal of Faculties and Universities. While clear in its initial motivations, as is evident from some of the sensible statements that introduce the final report, the operation itself was muddled in its objectives and decisions. Therefore, it once again left room for misunderstandings and reproduced, at a new level, the same game of conformism and power that had been identified and opposed in the Faculty Boards. The lecturers, who were all placed on an equal footing in a situation not yet clarified in terms of relations between parties, commitments, competences, aims, activity specifications and orientation of the school's interests, and so on, found themselves faced with the prospect of widespread corruption, in which aggressive behavior could bring the same advantages hitherto reserved only for the highest ranks. After having seized power, or at least its provisional simulacra, through alliances and conspiracies similar in all respects to the secret maneuvers of the academy's upper echelons, the problem was twofold: closing down the operation, on the one hand, and securing the students' support on the other. The first seems to have been resolved by now through the construction of an organizational platform whose solidity is secured by the school's more traditional pillars. The second, however, seems uncertain: the subjugation of the official student representatives, consumed by the back and forth of negotiations, is counterbalanced by the assembly's instability and diffidence.

Once again, then, the task of revealing the picture of a mystified situation rests with the Students Assembly. This situation can be summarized as follows: The students had called for everything in the Faculty to become *research*, and the lecturers passively consented; but this designation amounts to a simple facial contraction, a grimace with no meaning. Indeed, the old power games, the ways of using students as labor-power, of passing off personal convenience as universal objectives, return under a new nominal cloak; and so does the *ex cathedra* lecture, redefined as a stage of advancement in a nonexistent field of research and broadened to the epic dimensions of an audience that no longer comprises just one course, but the entire school. The reassured "independent" press can in turn reassure its readers: The revolution in the Faculty of Architecture is over; under the direction of the university barons, the recitals resume in the students' Charenton.[16]

The underlying issues remain unresolved, and one cannot genuinely believe that there has been progress, rather than regression, compared to the positions already reached during previous occupations. In the Faculty taken as an example, as in other Faculties of Architecture, the original clarity seems to have faded into intricate digressions in which one risks losing sight of the basic problems that are still at the heart of the university debate and on which work is still needed.

The sixth observation, as a proposal for how to take up again the issues that are at the heart of the disagreement, is therefore on the mass faculty, education, and research.

The Mass Faculty, Education, and Research

The mass University is not an enlargement of the elite University, nor is it tantamount to its simplification and dumbing down. The quantitative leap is matched by a qualitative leap, transforming it into a separate model that is radically different from the previous one. To establish a mass University, it is not enough to set up larger or more numerous classrooms, to multiply professors or assistants, to increase or thin out the number of subjects, to intensify or cut down working hours. What is needed is a structural transformation that modifies the relations between the parties, that readjusts the balance between participation, tasks, and responsibilities, that ensures the flexibility of exchanges and discussions, and that reinforces a cultural rigor.

The aim of the mass University is to respond to a different social demand than that addressed by the elite University. It is not a question of training executives for the ruling class, but of preparing operators destined to respond to the entire social context, hence, specialized for particular activities, but aware of the ends and consequences implied by their action. The same objective applies to a mass Faculty of Architecture. Its task is to prepare architects for the various levels and branches of architectural practice, so that they are able to work with different tools and methods for each level and branch, within an identical conceptual matrix.

The orientation of the mass University must be sharpened through the continuous exercise of critique, precisely because, for the masses, a state of permanent tension and contestation is needed to help counter the risks of agnostic behaviors manifesting both inside and outside the school. Even more so, the orientation of a mass Faculty of Architecture should be informed by criticism, given that its resignation to an accessory, superstructural, and decorative destiny risks confusing the authentic purposes of architecture, that is, its very substance and role in society. The organizational principles of the mass University are the open curriculum and the aggregation of courses by department. The departments break the traditional separation of subjects and establish a real unity of teaching by anchoring it to a flexible interplay of different cultural tensions, rather than a static and predetermined configuration. These different tensions are encouraged to converge by the internal logic of the whole and by external stimuli coming from the social context. Within this unity, students shall be able to move by choosing their path according to their inclinations, with minimal waste and maximum cultural advantage, with the widest possible choice and the most precise decision-making responsibility.

A mass Faculty of Architecture must be organized according to the same principles, but with greater urgency and necessity than other more homogenous and definite Faculties. Architecture's state of heterogeneity and indeterminateness means that the department's function is firstly that of stimulating growth by maintaining connection to its original matrix; and, secondly, that of promoting excursions outside the field of architecture, whereby architectural material is seen through the lens of other activities, and the materials of other activities are seen through the lens of architecture.

Product design, building design, and urban planning, for instance, are different strands of a single field of architectural practice, which can be summarized as the transformation of a three-dimensional environment as a unity of physical space and the things placed within it. Each strand has specific aims and tools, and its own methodological developments, hence different sets of motivational and operational components. The department's task is that of distinguishing the different strands and the entire group of their components, of making them apparent and operational through a precise definition of their autonomy and mutual complementarity. It also has the task of following each strand out of its field to see where it intersects with other strands coming from other fields, in such way that these interdisciplinary convergences give rise to new types of activities: The strand of product design, for instance, converges with strands coming from fields connected with production; the strand of urban planning with strands from various disciplines that intervene positively or normatively on different phenomena of the human environment, at the level of territorial planning.[17]

Educational activity forms the backdrop of the departments, while the latter constitute articulations of research activity. The two activities are distinct but related by a relationship of mutual necessity. Indeed, teaching cannot be expected to encompass research, as has hitherto been the case in the Faculties of Architecture, since no matter how formative, it does not possess those intentions of discovery and inquiry that are proper to research. Nor can research be expected to include teaching, as has been assumed in the case of the Faculty of Architecture cited in the previous observation, since one cannot research without possessing the technical and methodological tools, as well as the appropriate scientific methods that enable systematic investigation within a certain discipline. For operational research, mathematics is a requirement; for research into the semantic transformations of the urban fabric, the history of architecture is needed; for technological research, knowledge of the nature and performance of materials is required; for design research, means of formalization that make possible the representation and communication of ideas are needed, and so on.

A continually updated didactic framework should thus provide the necessary tools to form a cultural foundation for research, which should be as broad as possible, firsthand, and of the highest level. Links to this framework should be included in the Faculty for all subjects appropriate to architecture, and extend outward, into the didactic areas of other Faculties, for all subjects appropriate to other activities but also directly or indirectly connected to architectural education. For nothing is more foolish than teaching sub-mathematics for architects, when there is just *one* mathematics already taught at the highest level in Faculties of Science; the same goes for construction science, which is already taught in the most correct manner in Faculties of Engineering; as well as for sociology or economics, which have recently been brought to the Faculty of Architecture as a stopgap for flagrant urban planning insolvencies, with as futile an effect as that which would be achieved by teaching sub-urban planning to Faculties of Sociology or Economics.

It should be up to the departments to manage internal subjects and establish links with external ones, in relation to the needs that are continually raised through research, leaving open the possibility of change by subtracting, adding, or renewing. More importantly, departments should allow students to freely choose and decide according to their needs and without any obligation other than that arising from an awareness of their shortcomings identified when defining their curriculum and in the course of their development.

Thus, in addition to the aforementioned task of coordination, the department may fulfill the function of a concrete stimulus for transforming the University from the inert aggregation of self-sufficient and incompatible Faculties that it is today, into an open, intercommunicating, and flexible *school of studies*; a school that is a place of multiple opportunities for study with students freely following their own path, liberated from all the classificatory preconceptions that split the unity of culture, free from the constraints of obligatory routes, and already stimulated to exercise their critical faculties in the autonomous and responsible choice of their educational path.[18] With regard to research activity, it seems necessary, in the current circumstances, to specify three obvious premises.

The first is that the research activity of a mass Faculty is the sum of numerous group research projects. This means that the group size must always be commensurate with the intrinsic needs of the research and that, regardless of the topic explored, the main requirement is the continuous and direct exchange of opinions and experiences between the group's participants. It is false and misleading to suggest that in a mass Faculty, research should be conducted by huge groups to give as many students as possible the opportunity to participate. Furthermore, it is suspicious when the group is led by a single professor, and possibly divided into subgroups whose coordination is entrusted to assistants or aides, with the result of reproducing the identical conditions of traditional courses, so reintroducing the same old merchandise and the same old oppression under a different name.

The second premise is that the research conducted in a mass Faculty must be oriented around a precise goal. Within a discipline many topics can be investigated, but some are more appropriate than others to scholarship. Since the University can provide a service based more on intelligence than funding, research that involves high financial expenditure, but low intellectual potential should not be taken on. It is not useful if quantitative research on traffic flows is conducted within a Faculty of Architecture, since this is better done by motorway companies or automobile factories. Nor is it useful if it carries out research on the conditions of housing or urban services, since these are more effectively performed by municipal administrations or building authorities. Instead, the University can take on those investigations that others cannot or do not want to pursue, either because they lack the intellectual capacity necessary to tackle them or because they know that the findings uncovered through the inquiry would undermine their own rationale.

This is, in fact, the crucial function of research and of the University as a whole. In the present circumstances, they can be nothing other than a catalyst for a different way of facing reality in order to penetrate it, innervate it with criticism, and direct it toward radical transformation. In view of such a function, the research undertaken in a Faculty should not consist of a random ensemble of subjects; rather, it should be oriented, both in abstract and practical spheres, toward the exploration of vital issues that need to be challenged first with heterodox interpretations and then with alternative proposals. These proposals should be so rigorous and explicit as to imply the various cultural and political responsibilities that pertain to such issues. This is the only way in which research can properly and truly become participatory. Other ways of doing research simply simulate practical common sense, empirical consideration, and attachment to the concrete, while concealing interested connivances through smoke and mirrors; in other words, they serve as props for the preservation of the system.

The third premise relates to the mode in which research is conducted and, in particular, to the type of working relationship that is established between students and lecturers in their working groups. This relationship must be strictly egalitarian, in the sense that each participant must have the same rights and duties with regard to the common problem of knowledge. Only then can the full force of collective work be expressed, whether it stems from fresh ideas or experience. Thus, group research is not only a propulsive framework for cultural development, but it also offers a concrete opportunity for developing nonauthoritarian behavior, presenting an example of democracy in action that feeds back into the whole structure of the school.[19]

Mass University, education, and research are therefore fundamental steps on the path of clarification that the Faculty of Architecture has begun to pursue, first with clarity and then with a fluctuating degree of uncertainty. This uncertainty is due to the ambiguity of the dialogue between the two parties. The students have resumed this dialogue, while realistically knowing there is no guarantee they will be able to purify it of all the obscure reservations which have caused a permanent lack of communication between the parties. Incommunicability is indeed the typical state of the Faculty of Architecture, so representative of its difficulties to require a brief seventh observation on

The Language of the Parties

Many external observers, who have participated in meetings between students and lecturers in the Faculties of Architecture, have noted with surprise that while one of the parties intervened, the other, lost in thought, distractedly waited for the end before resuming their discourse without the slightest regard for what the other party said. The two parties did not actually communicate: The language of each side, although apparently common, was in fact meaningless to the other, to the point that they took for granted the futility of listening. This is not a new situation for the Faculty of Architecture and (Italian) architecture more broadly. To some extent, it was already present from the days when teaching and professional practice came together in an ambiguous conciliation between art and technique to produce a servile and derivative language that annihilated itself in its contaminations. Yet, it has recently worsened when a new language started to pour from the professors' lecterns, devoid of grammatical and syntactical structures, and supported only by an intricate juxtaposition of phonemes borrowed from other disciplines.

The phenomenon is undoubtedly interesting enough to deserve the attention of linguists and sociologists, but even on the more mundane level of immediate observation, some elements can be discerned that help clarify the superficial motions of a context agitated by perennial contradictions. The adulteration of language derives in fact from a condition of cultural insufficiency that continually reproduces misunderstandings and frequently transforms them into instruments of threat and blackmail. The listeners who pretend to get the message for fear that declaring their inability to understand it might reveal their unpreparedness—especially those who regard their group as the most progressive and cutting-edge—are largely aware of this state of cultural insufficiency. But even more so are those who knowingly emit indecipherable messages, calculating the terroristic effect that their enunciation will have on receivers unable to detect whether such indecipherability stems from themselves or the messages.

Never has incommunicability been used as a lever of power more than in this case; so much so that the heap of phonemes has been followed by a piling up of corresponding graphemes: mechanically transcribed speeches and books extracted from tape recorders, like pawns thrown onto the chessboard of academic success. Through such misunderstandings, provoked by blackmail and fear, obsolete characters have retained their fame, and insubstantial ones have managed to achieve it by shrewdly spouting nonsense at a herd fearful of being shown up as ignorant, ready to nod along to the most absurd neologisms and outlandish word combinations, of the type found under the sofas of salons at the end of social gatherings. However, if we look more closely at the school meetings, where fortunately the nods come only from the academic side, it is noticeable that the students' language, albeit participating in the same unstructured configurations as the lecturers', reveals very different expressive and communicative intentions. The words chosen and aggregated, and the metaphorical meanings with which such aggregations are charged, show a progressive cultural tension that is inversely proportional to the regressive one of the opposite side. The two languages are certainly *unique*, as well as steeped in highly suspect admixtures; both are expressive of *internal* changes, which remain within the fringes of the elite. However, while for the students the expressions indicate an *internal* revolutionary transformation, for the other side they represent an *internal* reactionary regression.[20] That is, beneath a thick layer of apparent coincidences, there is a potential difference between the two languages: The students' disjointed phrases, so often ridiculed by a conformist press and public, are not the same as the lecturers' prattle. The former express an eagerness to break the walled partition that excludes a humanistic meta-culture from the transformations of the real world; the latter manifest a desire to reinforce it with buttresses of linguistic mystification designed to perpetuate the segregation of architecture and strengthen the power of its academic rulers. Moreover, this mystification is consistently repeated in the content of every message and every program devised to appease the most pressing demands; messages and programs that are either increasingly abstract, pointing to simulacra and models that are progressively alien and remote, or increasingly trapped in the banal pragmatism which the students reject.

What do these observations on language point to? They serve to prove that even at the level of linguistic expression, where they are constantly attacked, the students of the Faculty of Architecture endeavor to look forward, just as much as the other side persists in looking backward. In addition, they make it clear that in the Faculty of Architecture, for good reasons, a condition of incommunicability has been created that reinforces positions of power and makes the search for a solution harder than elsewhere. Both sides, despite the potential differences noted, are prone to the temptations of jargon. This jargon does not derive from the intrinsic and instrumental needs of formalization, as is the case in the exact sciences and, to some extent, in the social sciences; rather, it simulates and falsifies current literary language through a series of thoughtless admixtures and substitutions. As well as closing off the possibilities of contact with the outside world, as jargons do, this mystifying jargon also sets up internally those hurdles and initiation requirements that are typical of the academy. The result is a condition of isolation and conservative rigidity that spreads from the Faculty to the profession, involving both in the same crisis. The Faculty's ills are reflected on architectural practice and vice versa; hence I (provisionally) conclude with a final observation on

The Contradictions of Italian Architecture

Despite the insistence of crude and superficial propaganda, overall little *good* has been achieved in Italian architecture. Although a lot of noise has been made in a vacuum sealed off from the problems of contemporary society, rarely have any indications emerged that have moved beyond the realm of personal gesture.

It is well known that Italian architecture came very late to an awareness of that great renewal of commitments and images that goes by the name of the modern movement. It has been said that such a delay was a consequence of fascism; but fascism, in the form of architecture, was itself made possible by a detachment from reality that preceded the advent of political fascism upon which the responsibility for this delay was placed. Today, in fact, this lag continues and the detachment from reality, which is its cause, appears to be an inherent vice. Despite the metamorphosis of the political structure and some spirited initiatives coming from isolated innovators, the situation does not seem to have changed much. The old idealistic ruse of skirting around problems by discounting them at a descriptive level without actually addressing them continues to reproduce itself. In this ruse, the rationalist experiences of the 1930s, the neorealist experimentalism of the immediate postwar period, the expansion of technological and urban planning interests of the 1950s, the attempts made since the early 1960s to open up an interdisciplinary discourse to establish proper scientific bases to address the problems of the Great Number, were all reduced to ashes. Every novel radical movement, at the very moment of its emergence, was countered with a diversionary contortion aimed at reestablishing the previous order: International rationalism was countered with a neoclassical nationalism, neorealism with a fraudulent organicism, a commitment to urban planning with a communitarian arcadia, industrial design with styling, scientific methodologies with the recovery of inspiration, and so on. The continuous alternating of actions and reactions often produced by versatile players, adept at going through each phase in both positive and negative junctures, has reduced Italian architectural culture to a condition of hysteria. Under such conditions, there is a new flourishing of voices that rave about detachment from concrete reality and deliberately ignore the creative energies of democratic expansion, collective participation, scientific progress, technological development, and refusal as an active choice. These voices play with reproposing outdated revolutionary models in the full tranquility of an appeasement brought about by the passing of time; they concoct complicated, astonishing alliances to win power.

While the students express the pressing need for a renewal of an architecture that is fit for a more intense participation in the structural transformations of society, a new diversionary contortion supporting the idea of architecture as an *uncontaminated art* and the school of architecture as *academia* looms both on the other side of and astride the barricade. Once again, the image of a comfortable prostitution sheltered from the vulgarities of the real shines through.

Architecture's rationale is far more complex and challenging than the academic hibernation that is being proposed. Confronting the problems of the physical environment has become fundamental to the world's progress. For every economic and social planning action, for every political perspective, one can no longer disregard the structures and forms that the physical environment takes to make such propositions actual and concrete. This is why, from the matrix of architecture, urban planning emerged as the science of structural and formal transformations of the territory, and, in a similar vein, industrial design emerged as the science of the mass production of things that, by being placed in the territory, participate in its transformation. Architecture's field of action has expanded enormously, and its reverberations can be felt in many other fields; hence, specific competences suited to the different qualities of the objectives pursued and the instruments employed are now required. Above all, there is a need for new value systems and cultural structures that can upend the obsolete ideological assumptions on which architecture and society still rest.[21]

The great revolution that is looming on the horizon—with its profound excursions into the entire field of human relations, with its technological upheavals destined to upset general social attitudes, and with its new crowd of actors assailing the current system with corrosive criticism—finds (Italian) architecture once again unprepared. As in the proto-industrial age, the horror of taking on a responsible and committed role has given rise to a sequence of storms in the teacup of a rigid configuration. The students' revolt in the Faculty of Architecture erupted from the realization of architecture's uncertain fate. Indeed, the reason for its early appearance in the Faculty of Architecture, and for the difficulties it ran into there, was because the fate of its field was more uncertain and mystified than others.

Today, it is difficult to predict its developments, which are still open and in constant flux. One can only say that the trial has begun and that, perhaps, the pyramid can be overturned.

Why/How to Construct School Buildings

In times of crisis, such as the one we are currently experiencing, it is impossible to address the question "how" without first asking "why." If we were to start discussing now what is the best way to construct school buildings suitable for contemporary society without first clarifying the reasons why contemporary society needs school buildings, we would risk taking for granted definitions and judgments that may no longer hold, and our conjectures would be as plausible but unfounded as castles made of sand.

We will therefore start with four elementary questions in the knowledge that it is precisely these questions—which, because of their seeming obviousness, no one has asked for some time—that can help us discover the hidden signs of a new reality in the making.

- —The first question: "Is it really necessary for our contemporary society that educational activity be organized in a stable and codified institution?"
- —The second question: "Should educational activity necessarily take place in purpose-built buildings?"

—The third question: "Is there a direct and reciprocal relation between educational activity and the quality of the buildings in which it takes place?"
—The fourth question: "Should the design and implementation of buildings for educational activity be entrusted to specialists?"

The fourth question leads directly to the problem of "how," while at the same time connecting to the first question of "why." In fact, it can be more accurately formulated as follows: "Should the design and implementation of a school building be entrusted to specialists who were formed through an institutional education that has trained them to consider first and foremost the needs of the institution?"

The four questions can thus be envisaged as four points in a circular relationship, where at each point reasons for continuity or interruption can be found.

We will examine these questions one at a time, looking for the steps that most reasonably allow us to arrive at the problem of "how."

1. Education is the result of experience. The broader and more complex the experience, the deeper and more intense the education. The field of experience widens in direct correlation to the frequency of contacts, and its complexity expands as their variety increases. Ultimately, to ensure a truly profound and stimulating education, no type of experience should be denied: All

possible contacts, of whatever nature, should not only be allowed but solicited.

But institutions are organizational structures set up to achieve predetermined goals: Tthey cannot admit and solicit any type of experience but only those that serve the achievement of their goals. Institutions, therefore, limit education along with contacts; they institutionalize education so that it serves the institution, first to affirm and then to defend it.

During periods of expansion, societies rarely consider the problem of organizing educational activity. The problem arises when societies begin to generate institutions, that is, when they move from the phase of self-definition to the phase of accumulation and preservation. At this point, education ceases to be organic to the whole field of societal experience and becomes functional to the limited field of experience admitted by institutions.

For example: The Greeks did not have any real organizational form of educational activity until the late Macedonian period, the Romans until the consolidation of the empire, the Renaissance until the Reformation and Counter-Reformation. Moreover, all the revolutionary periods in human history are marked by long pauses in institutionalized educational activity. Instead, education takes place where the possibility of experience is most intense; that is, in the exercise of revolutionary activity.

During the French revolution, the real centers of public education were the clubs, the streets, the squares (and the guillotine scaffold); during the Russian revolution, it was the soviets, the factories, the ateliers (and the people's courts); during the still ongoing Chinese revolution, it is the liberation army, the communes, the Red Guards assemblies (and the *tatzebao*); in the Cuban revolution, it was the guerrillas, the worker brigades, the defense committees (and the combat battalions); and so on.

Yet, while these forms of direct and global education were expanding, the authoritarian and reductive structures of institutional education were already being configured in response to internal contradictions. In France, for instance, the Constituent Assembly and the Convention had already begun to lay the foundations of an educational system that served the objectives of the state apparatus; a system that was first taken as a model by the Napoleonic empire and subsequently by all modern states—regardless of their different ideological and political orientations.

Napoleon's definition of education as a "means of directing public opinion" sums up precisely not only what institutional education had been before him (conditioned by the power of religion or absolutism), but also what it would be afterward (conditioned by the power of capital or state bureaucracy).

Since then, in fact, the two problems of education and the control of public opinion have been inseparable—every need in the former opens up needs in the latter, and vice versa. The expansion of culture, which objectively increased the critical potential of the social body, made it necessary to have an increasingly articulated control of public opinion, which, to be effective, had to restrict the sphere in which culture is formed by organizing a rigid and unified didactic structure. The development of industry and technology has pushed this iteration to the extreme, generating both the need for mass education—to meet the demands of production and consumption—and, at the same time, the need to condition through a controlled school system the educated masses, to prevent them from becoming aware of their exclusion from the processes of decision-making and the exercise of power.

Specialization has long seemed to be the most appropriate expedient to resolve the contradiction of these two opposing demands. Its economic rationale, even if limited and banal, was enough to justify its alienating effects: The specialist only needed to possess the sufficient knowledge necessary to perform efficiently their role in a process that, for lack of a broader vision, would ultimately escape their capacity for judgment.

Today, however, this expedient that has worked almost perfectly for so long is beginning to show its inconsistency. The student revolt, which is now raging throughout the world at every level of education and is also spreading to professional occupations and trades, has revealed a resounding refusal of the conditions of exclusion that result from placing an aprioristic and codified limitation on the field of cultural action. The idea that specialization is only legitimate—and becomes indispensable—when it is configured as the pinnacle of a holistic and elevated field of knowledge is becoming increasingly clear, because only in this case is the capacity to critically assess—that is, to accept, reject or, in any case, chose and make politically active—one's role in the social context guaranteed. In this case, the principle of specialization/alienation tends to be replaced by that of specialization/participation, which entails the revolutionary overthrow of the entire existing institutional system, and, in particular, of the institutions intended for educational activity.

With the revolt of the youth, education has returned to the city and the streets, thus discovering a field of frequent and articulated experiences far richer and more formative than those offered by the old school system. Perhaps we are moving toward an era in which education and global experience will once again coincide, in which the school as a stable and codified institution no longer has any reason to exist.

2. Education has always been conceived as a segregated activity. Plato taught while strolling in the Academy Park and Aristotle in the precincts of the Apollo Lyceum, but this was, as we have seen, a still unorganized education. When education started becoming an institution, buildings were promptly erected to both contain it and, at the same time, isolate it from contact with the outside

environment. Monasteries were built in the early Middle Ages, the first campuses in the late Middle Ages, academies during the Renaissance period, theological schools between the Reformation and Counter-Reformation, and the first large university complexes under the Age of Absolutism. In the period dominated by capitalism and state bureaucracy, a great variety of school facilities were built with different configurations corresponding to different types and levels of education.

From the end of the nineteenth century to the present day, as the principle of specialization became established, specialized education and, correspondingly, typologies of school buildings have multiplied. Each branch of education has developed its own type of building, specific to its purpose and more or less differentiated in terms of organization and morphology.

But despite the precise differences in definition and the vague differences in configuration, all types have in common the strictest adherence to the principle of segregation. The school is a physical structure intended exclusively for education, teachers, and students, just as the prison is a physical structure intended exclusively for imprisonment, jailers, and prisoners; its function is to accommodate a specific activity and also to isolate it from other activities.

The motive behind this function is the preservation of the class cohesion and institutional integrity of educational activity.

Isolation within a unified place acts as a filter to experiences not permitted by the institution and as a barrier to classes that do not control it. We know that this model has undergone a series of deformations over time. The expansion of mass education has caused a torsion that has continued to tug at the bars of the cage without, however, changing its substance. In certain cases, the bars have been widened—for example, in the case of lower or vocational education—when the need for a large dissemination of learning centers made it necessary to assimilate them into the urban fabric. But the cage has continued to be a cage: The school building has continued to be a distinct and autonomous physical structure, a conspicuous point of discontinuity in the fabric into which it is inserted.

The representation of this type of teaching is clearly given in the very design of buildings, where closed organizational structures and monumental architectural forms are invariably present. However different their appearances might be, the organizational structures of a school building can be traced back to patterns based on the principle of authority: hierarchy of spaces, lack of osmosis between different parts, interruption and control of internal and external communication, and so on. The formal configurations, on the other hand, correspond to the authoritarian setting of the organizational structures, in which anonymity is compensated for with symbols and monumentality.

In response to the inevitable remark that such authoritarian and monumental features are more typical in nineteenth-century schools than contemporary ones, one may object that a series of classrooms serviced by a corridor is essentially equivalent to a series of classrooms connected to a common space, and that the monumentality of the columns and decorations made of concrete is essentially equivalent to the monumentality of steel frames and curtain walls. Indeed, in architecture, organizational structures can be defined as authoritarian when the articulation of spaces does not stimulate the community to engage in communicational exchanges at all times and on a level of absolute equality; formal configurations are to be considered monumental when they conform to the aesthetic codes of the institutions and do not accommodate the free expression of users.

In fact, in the contemporary period little has been done to change the features—authoritarian and monumental—that school buildings have always had. Whether in cities or the countryside, schools are immediately recognizable: They stand there, emphatic and isolated, even when they are embedded in the densest of urban fabrics. All the tricks devised to render more humane their formal expression have aimed to define an elementary and schematic language, as is always the case when the empirical idea of "people" (a plurality of individuals who give rise to a variable field of interrelationships) is confused with the abstract idea of "mass" (an amorphous aggregation of human units who are rendered so by the fact of being aggregated). On the other hand, all the measures put in place to reduce their isolation have proven vane, since the problem has been approached from the outside rather than from the inside, which is where the true crux of the matter lies. The fact that the school has been considered as the culmination of a sphere of influence, or even as a possible community hub, or that time limits for its accessibility and protections for its access routes have been established, could in no way change its status as standing "apart" from its urban or territorial context.

School buildings constructed specifically to accommodate educational activity can therefore only accommodate that part of education that is convenient for the institutions that construct those school buildings. The remainder—the richest and most active part of education—takes place elsewhere and does not need buildings: Or, perhaps, it has not yet found the appropriate spaces in which it can be fully realized within a framework of global experience.

3. Socrates used to teach in Athenian gymnasiums and, many centuries later, Pestalozzi began his work as a teacher in a farm in Neuhof near Zurich. In addition to these two exemplary cases, there are many others in the history of pedagogy which demonstrate that a school can be excellent even if it is housed in an inappropriate or downright shoddy building. Conversely, there are several

cases of buildings regarded as excellent which accommodate altogether poor schools. Therefore, there is no linear and reciprocal relationship between architectural quality and the quality of the educational system. After all, it is an obvious, albeit seldom recognized, fact that, given its superstructural nature, architecture can directly modify the environment but not the activities that take place in it.

However, we know that, by virtue of its power to affect the environment, architecture can indirectly influence activities, directing or diverting their ways of becoming actual through a complex play of feedback loops through which form and society are dialectically interrelated.

Yet, if it is true that educational activity today remains indifferent to the feedback provided by architecture, and if its quality, or lack thereof, is completely independent from the influences exercised by the physical environment in which it takes place—if this is the case even when school buildings are considered to be of the highest standard—then it is the very definition of that quality that needs to be questioned. That is, we should ask ourselves whether in judging a school building as excellent or poor, we are not resorting to an exhausted and conventional aesthetic code, which has now lost its universal meaning. Indeed, the aesthetic code that is currently adopted to measure the quality of a building—scholastic or otherwise—is the result of a long history of manipulations beginning with Renaissance parameters that correlate quality with an ideology of order.

But what is order in a formal configuration if not the expulsion of any expression that is inconsistent with the representational needs of the institution? And what is this expulsion if not a repressive act against collective participation, perfectly in line with the repression that those same institutions carry out in the political and social sphere? The correlation is particularly evident in school buildings where the principle of formal order that governs their architectural composition mirrors the principle of disciplinary order which is defined as the ultimate aim of education.

Contemporary school buildings—whether considered qualitatively poor or good—continue to follow the principle of symmetry, thereby reflecting disciplinary order in their formal order. Beneath the texture of a different language transpires the same compositional structure that underlies the architecture of medieval cloisters or the "barrack" schools of the late nineteenth century: clear separation of exterior and interior, additive planimetric layouts, rhythmic cadences of façade elements, monocentric sightlines, monotony of materials, technological austerity, decorative repetitiveness, and so forth. This compositional structure mirrors the authoritarian procedure of educating an elite so that they can exercise cultural control over the rest of society on behalf of the narrow social class to which they belong. Authoritarianism and the aesthetics of order are related products of the domination exercised by the ruling class.

Today this domination persists in different forms, but the contradictions generated by its own automatisms have begun to tear it apart at the seams. Education is in fact becoming a universal requirement; its effects are felt not only in the most advanced pedagogical currents, but even more clearly in the tensions that agitate the cultural elites themselves and, first and foremost, the students.

Even if authoritarianism remains the pillar of education, it is now clear that teaching cannot continue to be authoritarian for long. Accordingly, one might say that although the ideology of order is still the pillar of the aesthetic code governing the architecture of schools, it is now clear that the architectural values of the future will rest upon a radical revaluation of disorder.

The mere mention of the word *disorder* generally provokes irrepressible neurosis, so it must be made clear that disorder does not mean the accumulation of systemic dysfunctions but, on the contrary, the expression of a higher type of functionality capable of including and making manifest the complex interplay of all the variables involved in a spatial event.

On the other hand, order is obtained through a selective process that isolates only the variables deemed relevant and organizes them into a system which is as simple as possible; namely one that offers a stable solution. We know that there is an increasing tendency to organize physical space according to such a reductive principle. This is the origin of all the additive methods that are universally applied to the construction of the environment; for instance, the method based on the search for optimal typologies, according to which it is possible to excise activities from their context and attribute to them spatial prototypes—or series of prototypes—whose additive combination gives rise to an environmental whole: the street, the neighborhood, the city.

We also know that what catches our interest in a city, neighborhood, or street, and even in a building, is precisely all that which manages to escape the control of these rules, all the "unacceptable" expressions that slip through the cracks of order and reveal themselves with all the stimulating richness that is proper to contradictions.

The patterns generated by these unacceptable expressions give rise to an imperfect configuration of disorder; the configuration would be perfect instead if these expressions were admitted within a complex system that was from the outset organized to accommodate them. In that case we would be in a condition based on collective participation—on the creative collaboration of the entire community—which is quite different from the discriminatory and segregationist condition we are currently in. In that case the organization of the physical environment would derive from an open process and not from authoritarian acts; the solutions would not be fixed but in continuous formation; the aesthetic code would not be exclusive and secret, but inclusive and manifest.

Although we are still a long way from this condition, we are faced with the objective necessity of bringing it about. The salvation of the world—in all fields, from politics to aesthetics—lies in embracing disorder as an alternative to a constrictive and oppressive order that can no longer be accepted.

In conclusion, returning to school buildings and the problem of their qualitative transformation, the only possible way to ensure they exert positive feedback on educational activity is by overturning the procedures according to which they are designed and built. The school should not be an island, but part of the broader physical context, which should itself be conceived as a whole and in relation to educational needs. It must not be a closed arrangement, but a structure which branches out into the fabric of social activities, capable of articulating itself with respect to their continuous variations; it must not be an object presented according to the rules of a preestablished aesthetic code, but an unstable configuration that is continually recreated through the direct participation of the community that uses it and is open to the disorder of its unpredictable expressions.

4. Collective participation in the shaping of the environment implies radical changes in the role of the architect.

If we agree that all expressions should be admitted even if they give rise to situations of disorder; if we establish that these situations of disorder are legitimate even if they contrast with the official aesthetic code founded on an ideology of order; if we attribute to disorder an internal logic that has not yet been revealed only because it is complex and therefore exceeds the elementary schemes that we have become accustomed to handling; if we accept that the impulses which lead to the definition of an environmental configuration must freely interlink in a process that continuously generates new solutions; if we consider all this as consistent with the most progressive tendencies of society and therefore desirable, then the function of the architect must change in the same way that the functions of all specialists working in various professional fields must change.

First and foremost, the motivations and aims of the profession are at stake. The profession of the architect—like that of all professionals—is defined and delimited by the mandate with which institutions entrust them to carry out a specialist activity on their behalf, based on the implicit commitment that they will accept the institution's objectives in exchange for a relative freedom of choice with regard to the technical aspects of the problems addressed. The exercise of critique is permitted only so far as it is internal to the system and does not undermine the foundations on which the system is based.

In a state based on collective participation, the mandate does not come from the institutions but from the entire community, or—more precisely—it is no longer a matter of delegation but of an agreement that is continually renewed through ongoing confrontation. In such cases, not only is the exercise of critique admitted but it becomes necessary. It can no longer be confined to technical aspects but should rather be extended to all the motivations and consequences of every decision, based on a permanent review that always reconsiders even the most general objectives.

The scope of the architect's field of action is also brought into question. Like most professionals, architects tackle the problem they are tasked with solving without worrying too much about the repercussions that the solutions will have on the general context into which they are inserted. Either they completely ignore the entire network of interrelationships or reduce it considerably to simplify the problem or to elevate their personal interpretation to the highest possible level of abstraction.

In a state based on collective participation, the consideration of this network of interrelationships, which are established between any new intervention and the context for which it is intended, instead becomes crucial.

To design a school building means: designing a piece of the city, intervening in the city in a way that is consistent, changing the city to make it consistent with the designed intervention, intervening on the entire force field of the city, and putting it all into motion while anticipating the consequences of this movement.

Finally, the architect's methodology of action is called into question. More than any other professional, architects design projects that are closed and finite. They start from a given function that is excised from the wider context, then draw up a suitable structure to make it actual within these abstract limits, and finally they configure this structure into a physical form that stands in for it and makes it tangible. Yet, this procedure suffers at every step from the level of abstraction that was accepted right from the start when the activity was excised from the wider context thus severing its ties with reality. This initial authoritarian decision imparts its authoritarian charge on the subsequent stages, which in turn become authoritarian. Indeed, the drawn-up structures operate as exclusive organizational systems and the physical forms are configured as concluded and inflexible creations, which are presumed to be all the closer to aesthetic perfection the less room they leave for the vagaries of use and time.

The intended outcome—rarely achieved, due to a recurring technical imperfection, which makes matters worse—is minimum entropy, that is, to reduce to the smallest possible number the connotations of a designated event. This is the opposite of what happens in any spatial situation endowed with universal meaning and therefore rich in signs that accumulate and become stratified over time as a consequence of its continuous relationship with society.

In a state based on collective participation, organizational systems are instead necessarily inclusive and included as parts within a more general system that realizes the indivisible unity of all activities. On the other hand, forms must be necessarily open, that is, defined only by the essential elements that generate and regulate their evolutionary process. To design a school building for a state based on collective participation does not mean arranging a concatenation of spaces connected by a circulatory axis crystallized into a stable formal configuration; rather, it means organizing a place full of opportunities for diverse experiences and actualizing it physically in space through a formal system predisposed to accommodate the multiple and variable expressions of those going through such experiences. Can specialists design a school building in accordance with such a conception? Generally, they cannot and do not know how to because of two fundamental reasons. Firstly, because their professional horizon does not go beyond the circle of institutional demands: The inclusion of collective participation would push them toward a field of criticality that they are denied by definition. Secondly, because specialization makes them adept at designing in terms of autonomous and self-sufficient organizational systems and closed and stable formal configurations: They have been trained for this and thus identify this as their proper function.

Hence, only a few architects—those who have freed themselves from their specialist and professional prohibitions—can make an appropriate contribution to the requirements of a new educational activity. Yet, many more are needed to confront the enormous scale of the problem.

As expected, by attempting to address the question of "why" we have begun to penetrate the depths of "how." It is now time to conclude the analysis by focusing on the consequences in terms of actions, without, however, going beyond the enunciation of a few general guidelines. In fact, any prescriptive norm would be vain and contradictory with respect to the mobile panorama that has emerged. From this perspective, we shall thus revisit some of the main issues in the same order in which we considered them thus far.

1. Institutional schooling provides a limited education because it grants only those experiences permitted by the institution and excludes all others. However, forbidden experiences are quite often the richest for learning, if only because they contain germs of refusal that stimulate critical activation.

Che Guevara maintained that the whole of society should be an immense school; and he was right, insofar as we understand—as he did—that society should not be organized on the existing institutional bases, nor on any other bases that produce the same authoritarian and discriminatory situations as the existing institutions.

The experiences that the institutions do not permit can only be obtained in the city and the territory, where they coexist with permissible experiences and insinuate themselves into their fabric, tearing it apart with the contradictions of concrete reality. As we wait for societal change, the city and the territory present an immense school that is already at our disposal. We must then work with energy and imagination so that the school becomes one with the city and the territory, so that the immense growth in demand for education, typical of the current conjuncture, can spread to the city and the territory.

The design of schools purged of institutional limitations must begin with the noninstitutional design of the physical environment.

2. The least suitable place for education to take place in is the school building. This is due to the fact that, by confining teaching and learning to an isolated and closed unitary space, the school building tends to cut off contact with the complex context of society. At the same time, the demands of mass education have led to the accelerated proliferation of educational structures. It is then imperative to reconcile these two opposing demands, which either deny or confirm the usefulness of schools, recommending either their elimination or multiplication. The only possible solution can be the disintegration of the school building as a specific place destined exclusively for a specific function.

It is a matter of distinguishing between the essential "core" of education, which must be preserved and multiplied, and its nonessential "ring," which, given how it furthers the unacceptable objectives of autonomy and exclusion, should be shattered and dispersed. Education consists of the search, which is potentially identical for both students and teachers, for knowledge and attitudes that enable each individual to find their appropriate role in society. The search for knowledge implies the existence of a technical apparatus (the core) that can be specialized; the search for attitudes implies the formation of places (the ring) where a continuous and generalized exchange can take place. To achieve the generalization and continuity of exchange, the physical structures of the school's ring must be spread throughout the city and the territory—mixed, superimposed, and integrated with other physical structures intended for other activities and thus generative of other experiences. To specialize the technical apparatus, however, the physical structures of the school's core must be concentrated and unified, while retaining the possibility of joining them to the structures of the ring and, through them, to the city and the territory whenever deemed necessary.

From this perspective, we can imagine the school as a twofold network stretching across the environment and consisting of both places where multiple activities unfold, among which education and places where the specific educational tools of knowledge retrieval, processing, and transmission are concentrated. The hubs of these two networks should not necessarily coincide nor be static, but rather they should be as distinct and mobile as possible, to always be located in the most germane conditions: the former where social experiences are at their most intense, the latter where specialized cultural services are required. The idea of a school structure made up of capsules comprising libraries, laboratories, studios, didactic technologies, learning models. and so on, which can move around urban areas to reach the places where groups of students and teachers live and carry out their research using facilities intended for other activities, is not unthinkable (and indeed, for other reasons and with different objectives, has already almost been prophesied).[1]

In this way, the idea of the school as a unified place, which results in exclusive organizational types and monumental configurations, would fall away. Education would in fact become a ubiquitous network, capable of penetrating everywhere and being continually penetrated by events in society.

Compared to such an image, it is clear how vain and mystifying the nineteenth-century program of turning the school into a reassuring and celebratory materialization of progress has been, or even the most recent, and only apparently more modest, proposal to endow the school with such a polarizing energy as to make it into a center around which the surrounding environment could spontaneously reorganize itself. The school without a fixed location, disaggregated and dispersed, appears as a more credible opportunity for renewal, if only because it proposes the destruction of its own organizational preconceptions as a model of a more general subversion that encompasses the entire urbanized territory and, through it, the whole of society.

The noninstitutional design of the physical environment is thus not only a prerequisite, but also a consequence, of designing schools purged of institutional limitations.

3. The omnipresence of the school in the city and the territory is probably far off, but we can see possibilities of it becoming immediately actualizable in the unexpected opportunities that appear among the gaps left open by institutional inefficiencies. In the meanderings of its superstructural existence, architectural practice often happens to suddenly run into these gaps: Its readiness to fill them with subversive architectural material, capable of shaking even the most protected structures, will depend on the intensity of its universal commitment. We can therefore consider this possibility as if it were actual and, to ward off any risk of abstraction, at the same time consider what is actual as very slowly tending toward the possible.

The introduction of educational activities into physical structures intended for other activities, as with the inclusion of other activities in physical structures intended for education, cannot take place without a profound restructuring of the entire environmental fabric. This implies an intense planning activity. But at what scale, with what procedures, and by what operators?

All scales, from the territorial to the minutest place of association, should be taken into account, so that the urgency and magnitude of consequences remain constant from the largest to the smallest. We know that the current organization of the territory and the city is not only not designed for contributing to education but is obtusely calibrated for the opposite: to standardize experiences, to flatten every expression to a baseline level, to conceal conflicts through the separation of all that can be contested. The emotional stimuli arising from the city and the territory (albeit more from the city than the territory due to their respective accumulation of contradictions) are still being produced in spite of such planning. It is then a matter of releasing, at the largest scale, this stifled potential of energy and letting it explode into a myriad of experiential opportunities. Design can pave the way for this outcome if it overturns the conceptual, organizational and formal assumptions it continues to passively accept, if it re-proposes in critical terms the purpose and goals of its undertaking.

If we adopt the idea of a disaggregated school, dispersed throughout the territory and immersed in the more general context of environmental structures, we are then obliged to verify the legitimacy of all the physical structures that have hitherto been deployed to actualize human activities in space. We are forced to question whether it is still reasonable to dissect the physical context according to exclusive types, each corresponding to an isolated activity—the street, the home, places for production and leisure—or whether it would not be more appropriate instead to reunify it, in a way that corresponds to the actual unfolding of activities, through the definition of new global structures (within which education disappears, having already been included in all its parts).

The same critical procedure also applies if we take the perspective of the minor scale and focus on the smallest place of association, namely the actual school building. But whereas at the larger scale the reversal involves proposing a target of integration that aims to restore unity to the environment, here it involves proposing a target of disintegration that aims to destroy the autonomy of the school as an antagonistic force to the unified reconstitution of the environment.

In the traditional organizational type, which dominates the educational sector, design must first distinguish the constituent parts and detach them from their conventional unity. However, there is no reason why classrooms, laboratories, refectories, auditoriums, gyms, sports and leisure facilities should not be shared—at least in part and for limited periods of time—with other activities, which, even if not defined as educational, do nonetheless provide education, via non-institutional means, much more than schools do. Either each part can be preserved within the school structure while remaining open to the use of the entire community; or they can be relocated to other structures while remaining accessible to the school; or lastly, they can be aggregated with other similar parts to give rise to a new organism that, in being simultaneously embedded within different structures, can offer fruitful opportunities for contact and exchange. Thus, whether working on a major or minor scale, we converge toward a single purpose, filling any gap that might suddenly appear at either end. The twofold pretense to either expect the renewal of the school from the reconstruction of the environment or the reconstruction of the environment from the renewal of the school is merely an alibi covering up for a lack of imagination or a desire for preservation.

4. The formation of a new physical environment oriented toward global education and the realization of new school structures projected into the context of social activities should not be conceived as products of authoritarian design. As we have already seen, the latter tends to exclude from its field of action a whole set of complex variables, to organize simple systems according to the parameters of an authoritarian vision whose aim is order. Its choices are categorical and its

procedures perfunctory. It produces monofunctional additive structures and formal configurations subordinate to the prerequisites of purity as prescribed by institutional aesthetic codes.

But if we refuse to produce finished objects that are already defined in every aspect at every scale and aim instead to organize structures that are articulated to make possible any integration of different activities into open and variable configurations, then we must resort to more sophisticated procedures and include in the operative field the totality of variables at play. In this way, design becomes a process, that is, an unfolding concatenation of events, the motion, direction, and temporality of which must be steered, corrected, and regulated, without ever restricting the free expression of the different wills involved, if they are legitimate and organic with the unfolding itself.

No prefigured model can be set as the final goal to be reached, and especially no morphological model. For form, due to its intrinsic capacity to generate feedback, constitutes in itself an indispensable regulatory component. It cannot be arrived at from outside of its development as a conclusion already set from the outset but should rather emerge out of that development through a process of verification that is renewed at every step.

Even more than these differences in method and operation, it is differences in content that distinguish authoritarian design from process-based design. In the former the relationship between objectives and choices is made within a limited and preestablished field of consensus, while in the latter it unfolds within the unlimited and indeterminable field of collective participation. In process-based design, it is necessary that the intervention of those who, directly or indirectly, will use the planned project has an impact at every stage, not only to provide the full picture of their actual needs and ensure that all choices are comprehensively explored, but also to introduce at a structural and formal level the powerful contribution of collective creativity.

We should not rule out, and indeed assume as incumbent, that in the future the process of designing the physical environment may be entirely governed by the community: that the course of its phases, from decision-making to the creation of formal configurations, may be achieved through a sequence of choices, reviews, and inventions that are capable of being self-regulated through a continuous polyphonic confrontation. At that point we would be able to dispense with the ambiguous and insidious function of the specialist (that is, the architect). But that point is a long way off, and the time it will take to reach it depends not only on how rapidly the emancipatory transformation of society occurs but also on how swiftly the exercise of freedom proves capable of destroying the barriers of alienation erected by the exercise of power.[2] At present, the architect remains indispensable, especially in helping accelerate the return of creative capacity to the community.

The design of schools—whether through the comprehensive modification of the physical environment to foster global education, or through the definition of school buildings—must take this perspective into account. It is no longer a matter of designing sacred enclosures, which are as outwardly eloquent and internally rigid as demanded by the requirements of a dominant authority, and as inert and inflexible as demanded by the imposition of a will to order; rather, it is a matter of triggering a process generative of multiple active experiences, and hence, of intense education.

The project is the process itself: its repeated transcription in spatial terms. It unfolds without ever reaching a conclusion along a trajectory shaped by those who set it off (the architects), which is continually readjusted by those who appropriate it (the students, the teachers, and the people who use it, even for other purposes).

5. The task of the architect who designs a school is therefore one of outlining an organizational structure that must spatially actualize the educational activities, whatever their complexity and their degree of contamination by other activities that they may adopt in the course of their development. Depending on the circumstances, intentions, and responsiveness of the case at hand, the organizational structure will either contain within itself the germs of the formal configuration that it will eventually give rise to, or provide the basic ingredients that

will serve to compose it, or supply the fully defined fragments through which its future developments will be articulated. What is important is that structure and form leave as much space as possible for future developments; for any authentic and significant educational project must be grounded in the community that makes use of it. The architect's work should stop at the definition of supporting frameworks—that are not neutral but charged with tensions—which allow for the development of the most disparate modes of organization and the richest and most disorder-inclusive formal configurations.

In conclusion, we might ask ourselves whether there are, in concrete or imaginary productions, any episodes pointing in this direction. The schools we see in cities and territories around the world are identical to each other and to the schools of the past: torpid reflections of an exhausted educational system. No novelty can be found—except for minor formal devices and distributional contrivances—even in the schools that specialist journals and monographs select as exemplary cases for public attention. Nor do any truly new insights emerge from the studies conducted by research institutes purposely set up to explore the problem in various countries: Radial, linear, nuclear, or even cluster layouts represent more or less suggestive twists and turns that fail to overcome traditional boundaries.

There are actually only a few episodes where, due to exceptional and unforeseen circumstances, collective participation has suddenly surfaced. Newspaper photographs showing the events of the student revolt all over the world have revealed a new kind of school architecture that no architect nor educator had so far imagined.[3] Interior spaces radically transformed with the introduction of new uses, improvised objects, and newly invented signs superimposed over the rigid emblems of the authorities, colorful and irreverent tears in the gray and austere expressions of order, façades disrupted with banners and boards used to communicate with the outside world, courtyards stripped of their decorative purpose and filled with activities and messages, the sprawl of such activities into the surrounding environs, a street invasion, the toppling of cars, dancing with the police, constantly and passionately interacting with people, and so on.

Architecture's Public

The first part of this paper stems from a presentation given in Liège on October 24 and 25, 1969, at an international conference on the theme: "L'architecte n'a plus d'audience. Quel est l'avenir du domaine bâti?" [The architect no longer has a public: What is the future of the built environment?]

Revolt and Frustration in the School of Architecture

When the university protests exploded—the most important event since the end of the Second World War—the Faculties of Architecture immediately found themselves in the vanguard. In many universities across Europe and the world, students of architecture were the first to demand a radical overhaul of their schools' organizational structures and teaching methods.

Why? Because the Faculties of Architecture, more than any other faculty, had long been dominated by an

Academic Body concerned only with preventing new ideas (which in architecture were at least fifty years old) from seeping into the school. Since the school was the last bastion against the penetration of such new ideas, the conflict was harsh at first. The boundaries of the conservative position were solid and precise, so the prospects of renewal seemed equally solid and precise.

But after an initial period of stubborn resistance, the academic body began to wonder whether these new ideas, which it had always opposed, were really as dangerous as it had imagined, especially since they were now accepted by everyone—at all levels of power, even by the state bureaucracy and by real estate speculators. Precisely because of this universal legitimacy, a suspicion began to dawn that these new ideas had already lost their aggressiveness, along with their youth. Once reasonably persuaded of this, the academic body decided to perform an admirable pirouette, changing routine without moving the axis of rotation. By accepting the most innocuous elements of a new language—and possibly by introducing a few new characters chosen from amongst the most innocuous proponents of those innocuous ideas—they could better defend the old content they wished to maintain.

The operation seemed promising; after all, it had already been accomplished successfully in real estate speculation—albeit, admittedly, over a longer period of time and in different circumstances. Instead, it was a complete failure.

Why? Because in the meantime the students, who had grown wiser in the course of their struggle, had changed their perspective. They had realized that it was not just a question of organizational structures and teaching methods but was rather about the purpose of their preparation or, in other words, their social role. The objective of their struggle could no longer be simply to replace some symbols with other symbols, or some people with other people. Instead, it was a question of rediscovering why and how to be an architect in a world in which the symbols and people representing apparently opposing sides were both accepted; a world which by then the students, for good reasons, totally refused.

The key question was to find a different way of doing architecture to build a different world (we all know what kind of world this would be, but for clarity it is perhaps best defined in the negative: not classist, not racist, not violent, not repressive, not alienating, not specialist, and not homogenizing). For architecture to regain a progressive role, it was necessary first to verify what was actually new in what had been passed off as such, and then to build something truly, wholly new in content as well as in expressive forms.

This has not happened, however, and perhaps it has not even begun. The excellent premises which had fed the uprising faded into a state of general confusion, displacing the Faculty of Architecture from its avant-garde position to an inconclusive and frustrating rearguard.

Why? Because there was nothing either inside or outside the school of architecture or in architectural practice more broadly that could nurture a daring exploration. There was no line of thought or collection of facts sufficiently consistent with reality to form a matrix of concrete alternatives for modifying that reality. The field of architecture remained amorphous and impalpable, devoid of any trace of a structure. Not only was it incapable of regenerating itself, but it also remained impervious to the prompts solicited by its own contradictions.

The Ambiguities of the Architect's Role

Any discussion of the credibility—or the historical legitimacy—of architecture in the contemporary world must inevitably set out from the acknowledgment of this situation, taking it as the starting point of any investigation of architecture's future or past.

We shall then begin defining the inconsistency between the field of architecture and the facts of reality by examining the behavior of its protagonist: the architect.

No other connotation of human craft has had such wide and ambiguous meanings as that of the architect. The term has been used to refer to figures ranging from the head mason to god (supreme "architect" of the universe).

This boundless latitude of meaning has weighed heavily on the destiny of those who have proudly identified with the title, trapping them between the frustrating suspicion of amounting to the lowest and the euphoric vanity of achieving the highest. In different historical epochs, depending on the role that political power has given him, the architect has either been more of a head mason or more of a god; if not exactly a head mason, he was certainly a foreman, as for example at the end of the Middle Ages and the beginning of the Renaissance; if not exactly god, then he was a high priest and custodian of state secrets, as in ancient Egypt between the First Dynasty and the conquest of Alexander.

In any case, in all epochs, whatever the importance of his role, the architect has been under the sway of those in power. Since money, materials, land, and authority to act were necessary, and since the ruling power was the only force capable of furnishing him with such means, the architect by definition had to identify himself with the latter, even to the point of turning into one of its operational appendages.

Bourgeois society, famous for arranging everything and leaving little room for manifestations of independence to creep in, tried further to categorize the role of the architect by framing it within the more general concept of profession. As a professional, the architect became a representative of the ruling class. His duties were limited to the study and application of building techniques (later of urban planning and later still—albeit with incredible ambiguities—of environmental planning). In the performance of these duties, he found both dignity and economic reward; that is, as long as he did not worry about motivations and consequences—or, in other words, as long as he did not relate his activity to a more general political condition.

Thus, with the rise of bourgeois professionalism, architecture was thrust into the realm of specialization, where only the problems of "how" matter, while the problems of "why" are considered as solved once and for all.

However, the subjugation that was so successful for most human activities could not succeed with architecture. This was not because architecture had a conceptual and operational structure that made it resistant to instrumentalization but, on the contrary, because it had no structure at all. We should not forget that when the sacred program of specialization began to assert itself in a world shaken by the first tremors of the industrial revolution, militant architecture remained obsessed with style, believing that an eclectic manipulation of language could solve problems, which required instead a profound subversion of concepts and methods.

After all, how and in what could architecture have specialized? The very school for the preparation of architects was born from an ambiguous coupling of art and technique, which was destined to beget a sterile species. Its composition—which remains almost unchanged to this day—derived from the grafting of a few peripheral branches of the Polytechnic onto the old trunk of the

Academy of Fine Arts; that is, from a combination of irreconcilable contrasts.

The academic artistic background was destined to systematically cancel out the formation of any concrete proposition connected with technique, while, in turn, the technical focus was destined to trivialize any abstract expressive proposition connected with art. Forced into inorganic coexistence, both academic art and applied technique ended up delaying the scientific transformation of the architectural discipline and furthermore interrupted its contacts with social transformations.

Thus, the lack of a disciplinary structure saved architecture from specialization but, at the same time, threw it into a state of ignorance and vagueness that is at the root of its contemporary ills.

The Modern Movement: Between Commitment and Non-commitment

At this point, one might object that there was the modern movement, which produced many ideas and many heroes. And it is a legitimate objection: the modern movement represented an important chance for cultural renewal in architecture.

But we need to consider architecture's "credibility," that is, its capacity to have a "public." Therefore, we must start by addressing a question that today seems fundamental: Who is architecture's public? The architects themselves? The clients who commission the buildings? Or the people—all the people who use architecture?

If the third hypothesis is true—that all the people who use architecture are its public, a claim that appears unequivocally true today—then the presence and work of the modern movement and its heroes needs to be framed from a different perspective to the one fabricated by its publicity machine. We cannot escape the fact that the modern movement has retained substantial defects of the amorphous condition from which it emerged. For example, it retained the ambiguity of the role it had assumed in setting itself up as a bourgeois profession and by seeking to reconcile art and technique through a simple qualitative modification of the first of these two factors—merely substituting modern art for academic art. Instead, it should have moved beyond this superfluous dilemma through a reversal of architecture's objectives and methods, opening it to both a scientific turn and a radical expressive renewal.

But this was only the consequence of a more serious inheritance bequeathed to the modern movement by the amorphous matrix from which it had emerged: the deliberate and programmatic attitude of an elite.

This is not a criticism of the size of the group—as it seems indisputable that only small groups can trigger processes of actual renewal—but rather of the group's choices in defining their field of operation. The field that the modern movement set out to, and did in fact, conquer was already occupied by academic and mercenary architecture; a field restricted to relations between clients, entrepreneurs, landlords, critics, connoisseurs, and architects; a field built on a network of economic and social class interests and held together by the arcane tensions of a class-based cultural and aesthetic code; a field that excluded everything in economic, social, cultural, and aesthetic terms that was not shared by the class in power.

It is true that some of its "heroes" pursued visions and created works that transcended these limits, but while they may have toyed with abandoning their elite positions, they never actually stepped out to stand on the other side: the side of the people—all the people—who use and are subject to architecture. The ideas and accomplishments of these "heroes"—the likes of, say, Loos, Le Corbusier, or a few others who stand out from the rest of the movement (even though official criticism, in its glib celebrations, tends to bunch them all together)—have an inestimable value that architecture can no longer do without. Nevertheless, they made only a tiny dent in the huge mountain of unsolved problems that beset the contemporary human environment. By distancing itself from the real context of society and its more concrete environmental needs, the elitist attitude of the modern movement ended up accentuating the superfluity of architecture. In addition to the long-term shortcoming of its ambiguous professional condition, this estrangement from reality further plunged architecture into a condition of indeterminacy. If, on the one hand, this has favored the formation of a few great free spirits who embarked on an audacious search for the new, on the other, it has encouraged the formation of their opposite: a multitude of generalists destined to nullify the innovations of the former by reducing them to inert symbols entirely commensurate with the needs of the ruling class.

There is little need to describe this multitude in detail; they form the many layers of cultural activity: the philosopher, economist, sociologist, politician, historian, educator, technician, artist; the designer, interior decorator, graphic designer, builder, urban planner, and so on. Underneath these many layers, we find the bedrock of power: the expert developer, the rigger of building regulations, the cultural legitimator of the robberies on the city and the territory engineered by financiers, politicians, and bureaucrats to the detriment of the community, and so forth.

To describe these characters further seems redundant, as the public is already familiar with them, if only on a literary level, through novels, comedies, films, and TV sketches which present them as a stereotype of the intellectual alienation typical of our neocapitalist age.

Although this may also explain why architecture has lost its "credibility," it is worth analyzing the phenomenon at its roots rather than by looking at its branches, however dense and proliferating they might be.

The point is that "credibility" was lost when modern architecture chose the same "public" as that of academic and mercenary architecture, that is, when it assumed an elite position by siding with clients instead of users.

Historical experience has taught us that the elites, even when they claim to be neutral, end up being attracted to the forces that benevolently grant such neutrality because they know that it serves the instrumental purpose of hiding their own interested involvement. Indeed, this process of conditioning begins to take effect at the precise moment when neutrality is assumed. For when "neutrally" pursuing the problems of "how," the problems of "why" are forgotten.

Faith in "How" and Ignorance About "Why"

Two examples taken from the history of the modern movement are particularly representative of this forgetfulness. The first is the CIAM conference held in 1929 in Frankfurt devoted to the theme of "Minimum Dwelling"; the second is the CIAM conference held in 1951 in Hoddesdon on the "Heart of the City."[1] Certainly, the former was much more important in terms of the seriousness of commitment, but both were equally important for the prospects that they opened up (or closed down).

At the congress in Frankfurt, the architects addressed the problem of how to meet, as quickly and efficiently as possible, the great demand for housing that exploded in every city around the world after the First World War.

The architects were right to take up this problem, but wrong to believe that it was their invention. It had already been invented and dramatized by the capitalist system which, having caused the large-scale urbanization of peasant masses to supply labor-power for industry without making the slightest provision for their accommodation, found itself caught in the web of its own contradictions.

The alarm was sounded with the slogan "more housing or less production" (which found its echo in the architects' more strident slogan "architecture or revolution"). The remedy prescribed was the construction, possibly in series, of the cheapest possible housing, reduced to the minimum tolerable floor area, a minimum referred to as "existential."

The architects of the Frankfurt Congress offered a series of brilliant solutions, competing in a race to reduce as much as possible not only the square and cubic meters per person, but everything that escaped the abstract calculation of essential physiological behavior. By focusing on the "how," they played into the hands of power; by neglecting the "why," they lost track of the deeper reasons for their cultural commitment.

Today, forty years later, we find that those proposals have become houses, neighborhoods, suburbs, and entire cities—palpable manifestations of an abuse perpetrated first on the poor and, later on, the not-so-poor. The proposals also became cultural alibis for the fiercest economic speculation and the most obtuse political inefficiency. And yet, the "whys" so blithely forgotten in Frankfurt still struggle to surface with clarity.

For it is perfectly legitimate to ask "why" housing should be as cheap as possible rather than very expensive; "why" should we make every effort to reduce dwellings to the minimum levels of floor area, space, and thickness of materials, and so on, instead of striving to make them spacious, protected, insulated, comfortable, well equipped, rich in opportunities for privacy, communication, exchange, personal creativity, and the like? No one can be satisfied with an answer that appeals to the scarcity of available resources when we know how much is spent on wars, on building missiles and antimissile systems, on moon programs, on research to defoliate forests populated by partisans, on stopping strikers rising from the ghettos, on covert persuasion and the invention of artificial needs, and so on.

The hierarchy of priorities established by power has no other purpose than its self-preservation, and therefore no one can (or should) accept the low priority afforded to housing, the city, and the territory; nor can (or should) anyone continue to believe, following the dogmas established in Frankfurt, that is a good idea to design spaces based on the fastest method for cooking omelets.

Working on "how" without a rigorous scrutiny of "why" inevitably excludes reality from the design process. Proposing solutions necessarily lies somewhere between the definition of goals and the evaluation of effects. The refusal to correlate one's contribution with the two poles of motivation and verification is a typical manifestation of the idiocy of forced specialization, which also affects the quality of proposals and their capacity to resist attempts at alteration.

In fact, all the compensations that the Frankfurt architects had introduced to counterbalance the minimal dimensions of housing—more air, more light, more sun, more greenery, and more formal rigor—were progressively eliminated in practice as useless accessories or frills, symptoms of "abominable" ornament. They were not included among those "concrete goals" that the architects had failed to investigate, nor did they appear in those "concrete controls" that neither the architects nor the users could object to. Not only had the problem been badly defined, but its solutions were destined to cause the disaster which now confronts us. So badly was the problem defined that today, forty years later, although it is universally accepted that housing for the less affluent classes can be the cheapest and therefore most squalid product on the market, the demand for housing is still far from being satisfied. On the contrary, it represents the greatest scarcity of our time.

At Hoddesdon, as in Frankfurt, but with Less Intelligence

At the 1951 Hoddesdon Congress, the architects thought they had invented the problem of rehabilitating Urban Centers. Confronted with the squalor of peripheral neighborhoods and the desolation caused by the criteria of functional specialization which they themselves had proposed with the practice of "zoning," they had the sudden idea of entrusting again the Center with those opportunities for exchange, communication, choice, and emotions that the city as a whole had by now lost; of transforming it into a "heart" capable of pumping blood back into exhausted and disjointed urban limbs.

At Hoddesdon, as in Frankfurt—but, admittedly, in a wearier tone—numerous proposals were made: to concentrate the most important administrative operations in the Center; to channel the most attractive leisure activities toward it; to pedestrianize it; to construct huge car parks in the Center; to preserve its historic character; to concentrate tertiary activities and to open parks in it, etc. But as in Frankfurt, this invention had already been devised elsewhere; and in any case, without investigating motives and consequences, the need for action was unthinkingly embraced. By this time, landowning capital and state bureaucracy, united together in their interests, were already preparing the heinous operation that would go by the name of "urban renewal." In North American cities, where the wealthy classes had moved to the suburbs, the excessive commutes through congested roads and the isolation in an environment that offered nothing but the monotonous repetition of itself began to take its toll. In European cities, the wealthy classes had remained in the most valuable urban zones, so it was the obsolete state of the increasingly dense and expanding surrounding areas, occupied by less affluent classes, that began to take their toll. But in both cases the most irresistible attraction was the potential value of the building areas, well located in the center of the region, the outskirts, and the city, and therefore highly profitable once cleared of everything poor and socially unseemly: blacks or southerners, immigrants or the lumpenproletariat, foreign workers or, indeed, workers of any kind.

The architectural exercises of Hoddesdon once again provided cultural justification to an operation of economic and political plunder. The theories and proposals on the "heart of the city" would eventually lead to all that was said and done in the following years, contributing to the transformation of Urban Centers into Corporate Centers, Commercial Centers, Administrative Centers, Leisure Centers, or simply Historic Centers, a process that, with heartfelt rhetoric, was destined to preserve the patrimony of values and the privileges of environmental well-being of the ruling classes. Architecture's lack of reflection on—or congenital irresponsibility toward—its own motives and effects, contributed decisively to the expansion of social inequity in its most ferocious and shameful aspect: the segregation of classes in physical space. Whereas the center was reserved for the houses of the rich, for the most profitable economic activities, for bureaucracy and politics, the poor, in their minimal housing, were excluded to the outskirts and marginalized from the real life of the city.

Good Reasons for the Noncredibility of Architecture

The two examples of Frankfurt and Hoddesdon are drawn from the history of the best architectural movement, and certainly more serious issues could be uncovered by retracing the vicissitudes of secondary movements or large professional associations. However, the purpose of this analysis is not to accumulate evidence but rather to uncover the reasons for the crisis of "credibility" that has hit architecture today and to demonstrate how they have deep roots that need to be exposed and eradicated.

At present it is sufficient to observe and describe a situation that we could summarize as follows:

1. The period of heroes, of palingenesis and universal solutions is over. Function no longer automatically generates form; "less" has ceased to be "more," and there is little probability of "more" becoming "less" again; utility and beauty are no longer two sides of the same coin.

Also over is the effort to bring research and action together into a coherent whole. On the one side, there is Craft, obtuse, repetitive and uncritical; on the other, the Academy, which regroups its forces while remaining presumptuous, pompous, and full of fanciful ambitions. Opinions circulate in favor of architecture as pure technique or pure fantasy, of the architect as industrious functionary of the real estate registry or as inspired creator of monuments. Architects await solutions from sociologists, economists, or geographers; yet, since these are not forthcoming, in the pathos of their improbable social position, they talk a lot about self-negation. But usually, those who practice self-negation in public, work for property speculation in private, thus earning the means to negate themselves without losing their composure. In short, there is much confusion in the ideological sphere of architecture.

2. There is just as much confusion in its practical sphere, where design remains as empirical, inspired, intuitive, and artisanal as ever, and construction as coarse, imprecise, and inefficient as it was in Ancient Rome. Since the issues of mass production and prefabrication have not yet been sorted out, a leap was made into techno-fantasies, and since it has not been possible to solve the quality/quantity dilemma, the whole problem of an architecture for the Great Number has been evaded by turning to either monumentalism or formal utopias. This has led to a great production of "proposals" for mausolea, megastructures,

universal or futuristic systems, and so on, designed mostly for art galleries, the press, and, in some cases, as ornaments for the demagogical programs of administrative boards and state bureaucracies. Meanwhile, the problems of territorial organization, urban restructuring, transport, housing, facilities, and the workplace remain unsolved, and many decision-makers already look toward industry as the only force capable of responding to the most pressing demands.

3. Confusion is even more widespread in the school, where the students' revolt uncovered once and for all the stupidity and indolence of the academic body. The crisis has been profound and serious but, as far as we can see today, without decisive consequences. The speed with which the professors ran for the lifeboats, leaving the sinking ship to the students, is matched only by the cunning of their return to power, back on the bridge to resume the voyage without been much concerned about its destination.

4. That leaves criticism and, as its propagandistic and worldly vehicle, the publication of magazines and weeklies.

Overfed by the crisis of ideas and actions, criticism travels an intricate network of roads (which for the most part—as in a labyrinth of riddles—lead back to the starting point). Two main tendencies emerge from this web. The first analyzes the vicissitudes of architecture through the behavior of its heroes, and, in their absence, tends to invent them, causing misunderstandings that take time to debunk. The second, by contrast, creates models of simulation borrowed from the figurative arts, human sciences, or literature, sometimes even from the jungle of intellectual paradoxes. This creates even more serious misunderstandings that not only mystify the cultural content and social responsibility of architecture, but also provoke monstruous mutations in the architect's habits. Proof of this can be found in the transformation of language, now often obscure and lacking in syntax, which is used to conceal the underlying confusion of ideas and purposes by playing on the terroristic effect of its incommunicability.

5. As for journalism, its decisive function in estranging architecture from its real context is well known. Apart from a few exceptional cases, there is no magazine or newspaper column that illustrates a piece of architecture in a manner that takes the user into account, that provides news about how that architecture actually functions in its daily existence; that publishes images—photographs or verbal documents—in which the people who use, transform, alter, and recompose the physical three-dimensional organism that they have been given are also present. It is as if architecture were merely a potential space and not a concrete actual place, made of materials and inhabited by people in a permanent and continually changing relationship.

So why should architecture be "credible" today? It is not necessary for the user nor for the client. As in the period of the first industrial transformation, in this new era of obscure forebodings and intense hopes, architects debate trifles and lose themselves in the void of a reassuring lack of commitment.

Architecture Is Too Important to Be Left to Architects

Nevertheless, the world cannot do without architecture. As long as a group of humans exists in physical space, the physical organization of that space will continue to be not only a fundamental necessity of existence but also the most direct and concrete means of communicating through materialized systems of self-representation. After all, the main raison d'être for human beings at this stage of their evolution is the destiny of voluntarily and deliberately transforming their environment.

It is precisely in dealing with the internal contradictions that develop out of such environmental transformations that the role of architecture takes shape. Today, this process has become ensnared in the coils of an intricate paradox: While human activities multiply, become diversified and ubiquitous, decisions about "where" and "how" they should exist in space tend to be increasingly concentrated in the spheres of economic, bureaucratic, and technological power. The role of architecture could be to contribute to the freezing or thawing out of this paradox, depending on whether it sides with power or with those marginalized and oppressed by it.

While it is certain that only the second choice allows for a concrete renewal of architecture, it is also certain that this choice will never be made by what passes for "architects' architecture." Indeed, architecture has become too important to be left to architects.

A real mutation is necessary to develop new characteristics in the practice of architecture and new behaviors in its authors, so that every barrier between maker and user is abolished, and so that making and using become two different moments in a single design process. Accordingly, the programmatic aggressivity of architecture and the forced passivity of the user must dissolve in a condition of decisional and creative equivalence where everyone—albeit with different levels of impact—is the architect, and every architectural event—regardless of who conceives it and carries it out—is considered architecture. In other words, this mutation must coincide with the subversion of the present condition, where to be an architect is the result of power delegated in a repressive manner, and to be architecture derives from a reference to class codes which legitimate only the exception, with an emphasis proportional to the degree to which it is detached from its context. The expedient of "not reading the surroundings" (so effectively exploited by official critics who use uninhabited, cropped, and even doctored photographs, or whose linguistic analyses exclude all judgment on the use and consumption of the event analyzed) amounts to an ideological, political, social, and cultural falsification that has no parallel in other disciplines.

Architecture Can Become the Material Cause of the Context in Which It Is Placed

It is unlikely that a radical renewal of behaviors and characteristics in architecture will take place any time soon, nor can it take place outside of a more general renewal of the structures of society. Architecture, as a typical superstructural activity, "depends" on the transformation of societal structures. However, it is important to clarify the dialectical terms of this "dependence" to avoid it being oversimplified and used as an alibi for conservatism and abdication.

Structural transformations open up potential space for the renewal of superstructures. But if this renewal is to become reality, it must occur in the superstructures themselves which, in turn, create room for further structural transformations. The new superstructures feed back into the new structural realities, giving their motivations concrete tangibility. In this, architecture has an incalculable advantage over other activities, for it produces concrete images of what the physical environment could be like if the structural arrangement of society were different. It can wedge physically perceivable and experienceable facts into the margins of choice (or into the wounds opened by contradictions) of the structural arrangement as it exists today. Nothing new can happen in architecture that has not first been invented and elaborated within architecture and in architecture's own terms. But this new occurrence, if it is truly new—that is, projected toward structural transformations—can become the "material cause" of the situation in which it is placed, feeding back into the structure and contributing to its transformation.

Thus, we cannot wait in the lair of architecture as-it-exists and hope for a social palingenesis to automatically generate a new kind of architecture. Instead, we must change at once the whole range of objects and subjects that currently participate in the architectural process. There is no other way for architecture to regain its historical legitimacy or, as I said, its "credibility."

Participation and the Scientific Method

Unlike all proposals for stylistic renewal formulated so far, to change the whole range of objects and subjects would open up a process in architecture which has no predetermined trajectories nor final solutions. Indeed, collective participation introduces a plurality of objectives and actions, the outcomes of which cannot be predicted. It is only possible to prefigure a line of tendencies and behaviors along which the process might be set off.

The evolution of society toward the abolition of classes, the demographic explosion and technological development pose immense problems for the organization of the physical environment. If architecture is to preserve its role, it must adopt clear ideological positions and precise operational procedures regarding these issues. These ideological positions and operational procedures are linked by a relationship of reciprocal necessity: For just as the vagueness of exploration based on inspiration and taste corresponds to the dependence on the power of the client, so the rigor of the scientific method corresponds to an identification with the real needs of the users. Identifying with the real needs of users does not mean to design "for" them but to design with "them." In other words, it means widening the field of participation to the definition and use of the project, introducing into the system a whole set of complex variables that could never be composed in balanced situations, except with procedural systems based on a continual alternation of observations, hypotheses, and verifications, that is, the use of scientific procedural systems.

On this point we must be clear. Therefore, it is necessary, first of all, to clarify the basic differences between designing "for" users and designing "with" users.

The Quality of Consensus and the Quality of Design

The first fundamental difference lies in the quality of consensus on which the planned architectural event must be based. In the case of designing "for"—even if it was possible to eliminate all forms of alienation connected to the external position of decision-makers—consensus, once achieved, congeals into a permanent fact. It can influence the conception of the plan but not its management, that is, the concrete life of the planned event. It is, in fact, denied at the very moment it is accepted. By contrast, in the case of designing "with," consensus remains permanently open to contestation. Indeed, consensus is renewed by allowing for confrontation along the whole arc of the planned event's existence and, reciprocally, it renews the planned event by adapting it to the demands of a common agreement that needs to be constantly reinstated.

In the first case, the act of design remains authoritarian and repressive, however enlightened the intentions behind it might be. In the second case, it becomes democratic and liberating, stimulating a multiple and continuous process of participation, which not only provides political legitimation to the planned event, but also makes it resistant to the wear and tear of adverse circumstances and the passage of time.

For instance, we know from experience that the urban plans for cities or territories always fail, even when drawn up according to the most conscientious analyses of the situation and accurate forecasts of its developmental trends, and even when collective interests have been closely considered. Failure is usually attributed to the intervention of forces that oppose the organic development of the community and are hence hostile to the "good plans"—a plausible, but not exhaustive explanation.

In reality, those "good plans" fail because the community has no reason to defend them. Since it did not participate in their formulation, the community cannot rightfully consider them "good" and is therefore not prepared to stand up for them. We all know of neighborhoods or buildings designed "for" users that in the shortest span of time corrode and crumble under the weight of a refusal from within. This refusal is typically attributed to either immaturity or incomprehension, and once again, this is a plausible but incomplete explanation. Neighborhoods and buildings designed "for" users degrade because the users, not having participated in their design, are unable to appropriate them and therefore have no reason to defend them.

According to a conventional line of argument, it might be objected that one's point of view does not influence the object, that inverting one's view has no effect on the actual configuration of the object and the contrasts that it is invested with. But, on the contrary, it is precisely the point of view that matters, and the fate of the object does change according to the perspective taken. Many recent events show how easily conservative positions can be disrupted when their hidden mechanisms are exposed, revealing both a condition of oppression and an alternative prospect for progressive change. In such moments, when the community becomes conscious of its situation, it takes direct action and steps in to change it.

The second fundamental difference between designing "for" and designing "with" users, a perfect corollary of the first, lies in the quality of the design.

Is it really necessary to point out that "user participation" does not mean that users sit down at the drawing board, or that they dictate while architects transcribe, transforming aspirations into images? It would appear so, since some seem to believe in this literal interpretation or, without believing it, promote it anyway, displacing the frustrations of their incoherent discipline with populist jubilation.

In reality, participation transforms architectural design from the authoritarian act that it has been up until now into a process. This process begins with the discovery of the users' needs, passing through the formulation of organizational and formal hypotheses before culminating in the management phase. Here, instead of coming to its usual close, the process opens up again in a continuous alternation of controls and reformulations that retroactively affect needs and hypotheses, prompting their continuous redefinition.

The three phases—discovery of needs, formulation of hypotheses, and management—not only occur sequentially but also have a cyclical relationship. However, each phase is fulfilled differently, and the possibility for their relationships being consequent and well correlated within the same process depends on the specific ways in which each is carried out.

The Discovery of the Users' Needs

The discovery of the users' needs is not only an important precondition for beginning the process but also a matter of fine-tuning basic choices. We can opt for an abstract idea of the user: Man, with the different symbolic connotations that the rationales and tastes of the dominant culture of each epoch attributes to him. In this case, the process of discovery becomes a technical operation aimed at selecting and classifying presumed physiological and possibly even "spiritual" needs. Or, alternatively, we can opt for a concrete social condition by identifying a particular user, for instance, those who belong to the social classes marginalized by power, in which case the process of discovery becomes a political operation. We know where the first hypothesis, which was adopted to a large extent by the modern movement, leads to the illusory formulation of a universal scale intended to summarize all human needs but which instead, precisely because of the a priori contraction of reality on which it is based, ends up mirroring the interests, values, and codes of power. The four functions of the Athens Charter provide a glaring demonstration of the inevitability of such a result. When calculated in relation to an imaginary "average man," the classification of needs opens up no prospect of substantial renewal since it does not consider that facilities for work, habitation, transport, and leisure can be of premium or poor quality—that is, entirely different from each other and in many respects opposed—if seen from the perspective of those with power or those without.

The second hypothesis requires more complex research. For when referring to a concrete social condition—for instance, that of marginalized classes—the identification of needs requires the concrete presence of those who have them. On the one hand, this requires the preliminary gathering of information and criticism to debunk the imposed value systems, dispelling the centuries-old alienation they have produced, and to stimulate a consciousness so precise and biting as to provoke the ricocheting of new information and criticism. On the other hand, it entails an acceptance of confrontation—in other words, the possibility of challenging the very cultural structures (experiences, values, and codes) of those who trigger the process. Since what will emerge in terms of new information and criticism is unpredictable, it cannot be fed into old models without jeopardizing the process and falling back into mirroring the values of power.

In fact, those excluded from the administration of power—and therefore from what is officially recognized as culture, art, architecture—are not larvae waiting for a metamorphosis that will permit them to benefit from the legitimized values of power; rather, they are bearers of new values, which already exist potentially, manifesting sporadically in the margins not already controlled by institutional power. These are the manifestations of "disorder," which always seep into the territory, in the city, in neighborhoods and buildings, mixing with the pathological dregs of "order," with which they are commonly confused. But while the pathological dregs of "order" stem from the exacerbation of an authoritarian and repressive condition that overrides its own rules by spreading in a state of amorphous violence, the "disorder" opposing this "order" has its own complex branching structure that, not being institutionalized, renews itself continually, constantly reinventing the images of a reality in transformation.

Thus, the discovery of the users' real needs ultimately means clearly exposing their rights to things and, at the same time, their rights to expression; it means provoking direct participation and confronting all the subversive consequences that this entails; it means undermining all traditional value systems, which, since they were built on nonparticipation, must be revised or replaced when participation comes into play and unleashes untapped energies.

The Formulation of Hypotheses

The phase of formulating hypotheses corresponds technically to what in authoritarian design is called "the project." But in authoritarian design, this involves translating into organizational and morphological structures functional and expressive objectives that have been defined once and for all, or which are easily pinned down according to an institutional, and hence predictable, logic of behaviors and representations. By contrast, in process-based design objectives find their definition in the course of the process itself: They are defined through continuous confrontation between the pressure of real needs and the images of possible spatial configurations. In this process, needs are refined and configurations perfected until a satisfactory state of equilibrium is reached, even if some instability remains due to the innate mobility of the process. Thus, the function of design is no longer to fix a partial interpretation of reality into a permanent and immobile figure but, on the contrary, to pave the way for a dialectical process in which reality increasingly expands under the pressure of images, which in turn become increasingly varied by including new elements of reality.

In other words, unlike authoritarian design, which imposes final solutions from the outset, process-based design formulates a sequence of hypotheses aimed at (and revived by) participation.

Each hypothesis enlarges the field of forces already generated by the previous hypothesis, and in turn brings about its own replacement by a successive and more appropriate hypothesis.

The sequence stops when a point of equilibrium is reached which enables the implementation—the materialization in physical space—of the last hypothesis deemed satisfactory. Thereupon it starts up again in the phase of management and use, along new lines of experience. The difference between these two modes of design is so profound, both conceptually and operationally, that some further explanation is needed.

Authoritarian design cannot question the basic choices of the event it produces because it takes as a given that they should be pre-decided upstream. In the case of a residential unit, for example, the resources allocated are considered invariable, and hence the standards corresponding to those resources insurmountable. It so happens that if the residential unit is intended for a wealthy social group, it will be designed to high standards, while if it is intended for a poor social group, it will follow low standards, as if the human needs of the two groups were not absolutely identical. The residential unit for the rich will have high-quality urban planning and building typologies, while the unit for the poor will have shoddy and oppressive ones.

Observing this phenomenon from the perspective of an explicitly superstructural point of view (which deliberately proposes to unhinge the connections between structure and superstructure, providing reasons and opening space for structural change), we can bypass with a single leap the whole gamut of objections that without fail would refer to the ineluctable mechanisms of the free market. After all, it is well known that the phenomenon occurs in exactly the same way when the market is regulated and the logic of capital is replaced with that of state bureaucracy. Besides, what interests us here is the definition of new procedures for the transformation of the human environment that are based on direct action and therefore independent, by definition, from all the alienating automatisms of production and power.

Returning to the example of a residential unit for a poor social group, authoritarian design accepts without hesitation the senseless axiom that resources should be scarce and, as a result, standards low. At best, technical cunning will be applied to manipulate addenda that do not alter the total sum: more green space but greater building density; more usable areas but less subsidiary areas; more service space but less interior finishes; or vice versa, and so on. These maneuvers are performed within a supinely accepted cage, and the vain negotiation of choosing between various obligatory paths occurs between the client and the designer with total disregard for the user. On the other hand, process-based design introduces the user as a fundamental protagonist in the operation, and thereby calls into question from the outset the legitimacy of the constraints imposed on it, including those on resources and standards. The task of the designer is to open up the sequence of hypotheses, expanding the image beyond the parameters of the framework imposed by the client: to show what we could (or should) have if, instead of moving within a condition of preordained subjugation, we allowed an objective confrontation with real rights.

In the case of architectural or urban planning programs involving poor social groups—the most frequent and, at any rate, the most urgent case—the task of the designer is, first of all, to re-establish with clarity the terms of the class struggle.

The sequential hypotheses that they should propose must first reveal to the consciousness of the users the brutality of the authoritarian models that have brought about their current condition. This will involve comparing them with the models they would be entitled to if the economic, scientific, and technological means presently available were granted to satisfy their real needs. The subsequent hypotheses should then begin to involve the users as protagonists in a progressive action of selection and definition of the needs which the operation must satisfy, until a precise definition of the architectural or urban image that is to be achieved is reached.

Management and Use

In process-based design, the project does not end with the construction of the architectural object. Instead, from that moment onward, a new line of development begins that is consistent with the preceding one but characterized by different qualities. The client and architect leave the stage and the conflicts are shifted to the relationship between the architectural object and those who use it. For this relationship to be dialectical, it is necessary for each side to possess aptitudes for change through a continuous alternation of reciprocal identifications and dissociations. While the architectural object changes through the transformations that the user imposes on it to adapt it to their changing practical and creative needs, the user also changes through the stimuli transmitted by the intrinsic quality of the architectural object.

In authoritarian design, only this second line of influence is at work, and it does so repressively, because the plan is commonly conceived assuming that it is easier, quicker, and more profitable to condition people than to condition the environment. Therefore, in the phase of management and use, the user must typically adapt to the architecture as to an inflexible cage and all tensions are resolved in superficial alterations that contradict the pre-established morphological order, without being able, however, to modify it substantially. At this point, manifestations of "disorder," which arise from the creative pressure of the users, are blocked, loathed, and even punished by those who create, support, and guarantee "order."

The architectural object becomes a materialized representation of the institutional reason that generated it; it becomes an institution.

In process-based design, as already mentioned, the implementation of the plan in three-dimensional physical terms is a tentative hypothesis. Its verification occurs through use and is therefore entrusted to the user who confronts the built environment in experiencing it. This experiential phase, which adjusts, subtracts, adds to, and modifies, is still part of the project: It continues until the point of technical or physical obsolescence, which occurs when the motivation that set it in motion is spent or when its tissues are exhausted and have lost all their regenerative capacity.

From the perspective of process-based design, the teleological assumptions that have hitherto diverted architecture from its more concrete material causes fall away. An architectural work has no meaning if dissociated from its use, and the way in which it is managed, or can be managed, becomes one of the fundamental factors contributing to the definition of its quality. As an empty vessel, it cannot represent itself or establish purposeful relations with nature and history; for its only purpose lies in its "fullness"—in the whole set of relationships it establishes with its recipients. Following the movement of these relationships, it continues both to modify and be modified by those who use it. In this way it integrates itself with nature and produces history, becoming itself, through the use that is made of it, part of nature and history.

Following this perspective, some of the subconscious tensions that have agitated the most recent architectural culture, such as issues of growth and flexibility, take on a clearer meaning. Faced with the evidence of the rapid consumption to which architectural organisms are subjected today, because of changes in the circumstances which dictated their initial programs, an effort has been made to find a solution by devising organizational and morphological systems in such a way as to permit additions and adaptations. But in the sphere of authoritarian design, these devices are immediately blocked at the point in which they contradict a structural and formal order that is by definition preordained and unalterable. The quality of the object is locked in a tangle of exclusive and confidential codes that admit no deviations except at the price of widening a network of communication, which is precisely their task to restrict. If an authoritarian project were truly flexible and open to growth, it would be possible for everyone to manipulate and understand it: It would lose those characteristics of ineffability and purity that support and conceal its classist purpose.

The growth and flexibility of an architectural organism are in fact only possible within a new conception of architectural quality. This new conception can only be formulated through a more careful exploration of those phenomena of creative participation currently dismissed as "disorder." It is in their intricate context, in fact, that we shall find the matrix of a self-generating and open formal organization that rejects a private and exclusive way of managing the territory and, through this rejection, outlines a new way of managing it on a pluralistic and inclusive basis.

By restoring to the user a creative role, we implicitly accept this basis. At the same time, the structural and morphological conceptions and the operational tools that have until now governed architectural production are thrown into crisis. The large set of variables that institutional culture and practice had suppressed come back into play, and the field of reality in which architecture intervenes becomes macroscopic and complex. Therefore, only the assumption of clear ideological positions and the application of rigorously scientific procedures can guarantee the definition of a legitimate political and technical framework. Then new systems of objectives can be set and new instruments of action can be developed to produce a balanced and stimulating organization of the physical environment.

The Architecture of Participation

I am the third respondent invited to present their personal interpretations of the problems that have surfaced, or are about to surface, in the architecture of the 1970s. Thus, I shall try to do so by taking my cue from the hypotheses that Jim Richards and Peter Blake have advanced in dealing with this same topic, in the same forum, before me. Jim Richards has masterfully taken stock of what is still called the modern movement in architecture. He talked about the goals that the movement proposed when it began to develop and showed how, along the difficult and winding path that the movement has taken in the past fifty years, some of those goals have either been achieved or missed, or even forgotten. He then identified three circumstances that are likely to change first and foremost the practice, but also the conception, of architecture in the near future: the spread of industrial processes into building production, the growing conviction that architectural activity is only one particular aspect of the global transformation of the physical environment, and the emergence of a methodology of analysis and intervention based on the formation of interdisciplinary groups in which the architect, depending on the nature of the problem, might be either the leading actor or an extra. These three circumstances are likely to have decisive effects on the future of architecture.

According to Jim Richards, it is quite possible that in the near future we might be faced with two types of architecture: the first, anonymous but heavily characterized by the generalized use of refined techniques; the second, personalized and left entirely, as far as the expressive and technical aspects are concerned, to the inspiration of its authors. The city could become a fabric of common but technically exact architecture, punctuated by exceptional architectural episodes laden with symbols or, in other words, monuments.

It is precisely from such a hypothesis that I would like to begin drawing out my arguments, which are perhaps less an exact assessment of the current trends and more a projection of my own hopes. After all, I am not an architectural historian but a designer of projects. Later, following the line of my reasoning, I will also try to pick up Peter Blake's assumptions about pop culture's influence on architecture and about architecture's newly achieved awareness that it can no longer interpret and represent the development of society according to "finite" architectural configurations.

I will say right away that in my opinion the architecture of the future will be characterized by increasing user participation in both its organizational and formal definition. Or—to avoid conflating what will happen with what I would like to happen—I will say that in my opinion contemporary architects should strive to ensure that the architecture of the coming years will be less and less the representation of those who design it and more and more the representation of those who use it.

To begin with, I would like to offer some thoughts on what is happening in architecture today. If we open an architecture magazine from any country to inform ourselves about what has been built in that country, we come across the representation of a series of buildings that have been photographed and published without people. The editor, the architect, and the photographer all seem to be obsessed with a nonexistent yet permanent concern: to eliminate people from the scene, as if they were germs capable of contaminating the event being illustrated. When one later reads the articles, notes, or captions, it becomes clear that this intention to erase the presence of people is premeditated and part of a strange and obscure conspiracy. Sometimes we might learn about the clients and their economic, technical, or aesthetic needs; but seldom is one told how the recipients use or will use the building intended for them: whether it corresponds well, poorly, or badly to their needs. The judgment of the work is always completely independent of the judgment of its use. The work is considered good, mediocre, or bad in relation to other values, which are generally figurative values.

If, instead of browsing through magazines, we turn to more enduring informational mediums—such as, for instance, books on the history of architecture—which should be less susceptible to the fluctuations of fashion, we will immediately note that this mode of judging works does not change. Nor does it change when we find ourselves in a school of architecture, or in a seminar with experts of architecture, or in one of the many lecture halls where architecture is discussed. The issue of who uses it is everywhere avoided, as if it were a trivial or impolite subject: the belief is that architecture, being art, cannot by definition be contaminated by the concrete aspects of everyday reality. Admittedly, this tendency to treat architecture and reality as a dichotomy, which is nowadays widespread in almost all branches of criticism and news media, has not always been the case.

In certain past eras, when magazines and books on architecture did not exist, but architecture was represented, all the same, through painting, people were not removed from the scene. On the contrary, they often appeared in the foreground, in the act of using the architectural event intended for them. They appeared as the real subjects of the objects created for their use. So much so that architecture was revealed as not only consisting of buildings, but of people and buildings together, correlated in a relationship of mutual necessity.

Incidentally, it is curious to note how painting itself, while depicting architecture without isolating it from the people who used it, also deliberately became contaminated with reality yet by no means lost its substance as art.

To give an historical point of reference, we might say that the elimination of people from architecture entered criticism when a romantic conception of art began to develop, which also impacted on architecture, that is, around the final decades of the eighteenth century.

But I am also aware of how imprecise this statement is, because it would be like saying that the bourgeoisie was born at the time of the French revolution, when in fact we know that it was born much earlier, possibly at the time of the early Renaissance. So, perhaps, it would be fairer to say that everything changed when linear perspective first appeared (individual monocentrism of vision) or when bourgeois philosophy began to assert itself (political and cultural domination of a single class over the entire society). However, at this point, I would prefer not to wade into an overly lengthy and complex discussion of the deep roots of our subject matter, which is outside the scope of this talk.

So I return to the issue at hand to address straight away a first objection, the most predictable among all possible ones: The modern movement was fundamentally concerned with people, for it gave enormous prominence to the problem of the relationship between form and function, that is, between architecture and its use. This seems undeniable. However, it is worth looking more closely at how the problem was addressed and what solutions were provided.

First of all, in my opinion, we should not forget that the modern movement was born in an era when intellectual progress greatly expanded, but also when interpretations of human and social behavior were greatly simplified. At that time, all disciplines of human thought and practice were intensely concerned with Man, treating this abstract figure as if it was a strictly individual subject and from an exclusively functional perspective.

Take, for example, psychoanalysis, by which I do not mean its clinical aspect. I do not believe anyone can doubt that the foundation of a science dealing with unconscious mental processes represents one of humanity's greatest contributions. However, it is only fair to raise doubts—and the most advanced contemporary psychoanalysts are the first to raise them—about the sociological and political aims toward which the acquisitions of this science have been directed. The idea that the origin of an individual's mental disorders is to be sought only in their personal affairs, as if the individual were an entity completely independent of society, could lead to no other conclusion than that the psychic conflict erupts between a sick individual and a healthy society and that the purpose of therapy is to heal the individual in order to reintegrate them into society; to enable them to accept social rules that, by definition, are considered acceptable. Hence, all rebels are automatically categorized as mad who must be healed, or if that's not possible, segregated. Or take, for example, ergonomics. Again, there is no doubt about the usefulness of a science that studies the relationship between humans and their working environment to improve it. It is inevitable, however, that doubts start to arise when ergonomics produces "Taylorism," namely, a method of organizing work and the working environment that aims to exploit workers as much as possible, specializing them to the point that they lose all comprehension of the purpose of their effort, and plunging them into a state of alienation that turns them into an extension of the machine.

But to return to our topic, let us take as our examples the city and the house.

Toward the end of the last century, when the phenomenon of industrialization first exploded, the idea that the city was also an instrument of production began to take hold. Complexity, which until then had been considered a great quality of urban life (and still is, despite urban planning), was seen as confusing; hence, research was directed toward its simplification. The city, like a machine, was treated as a set of distinct parts, linked up by a relationship of functional necessity: Each part was supposed to have neither more nor less than what is necessary for its functioning, in the same way as a cog must have neither more nor less teeth than what is necessary to turn the next gear. In this case too, the instrument for achieving simplification was specialization. Thus, urban activities were first isolated, then classified and hierarchized, and finally located in physical space in such a way that they appeared distinct, with no overlap.

While in the preindustrial city, work, leisure, circulation, education, entertainment, exchange, production, and contemplation took place everywhere, in the contemporary city (the one designed by urban planners), each activity has, or should have, its place; and if it does not, that becomes (for urban planners) an error, an unbearable "functional inconsistency."

The principle of city specialization was not actually invented by the modern movement, but by German urban planners who, at the end of the nineteenth century, had found "zoning" to be the most suitable tool for bringing "order" (note the choice of word) to urban development.

Zoning was a highly efficient instrument, precise and at the same time adaptable to the most diverse circumstances. It was because of these qualities that, after Germany, it became popular in England, then in the United States and eventually in all more or less industrialized countries. With each step it gained new instrumental capacities, but also new purposes. Its original task of controlling building to avoid urban congestion was expanded with additional tasks, such as the regulation of the density and distribution of the population, the productive organization of land use, the guarantee of stability in real estate values, the establishment of a direct correspondence between the quality of different urban sectors and the economic and social status of their inhabitants, and so on. Thus, zoning ended up becoming a sort of ideological imaginary: projecting an ideology of production onto the urban scene. After having been subjected to the same process of eliminating anything considered superfluous to a system of rational production—premised on maximum output, minimum effort, and the reinforcing of economic and social stability—the city was turned into a machine (and a commodity at the same time).

When the modern movement began to tackle the problems of urban planning, it inherited this vast legacy and took it to its extreme consequences.

In one point, however, zoning was not successful in creating physical configurations as controlled as the technical and legislative prescriptions it had developed. After having stripped them of all the intersections, overlaps, and contaminations that characterized the preindustrial city, it classified and ordered urban functions according to simple systems. Yet, it failed to transform these simple systems of functions into equally simple systems of forms.

Motivated by a concern not to lose all the formal wisdom of the ancient cities, Camillo Sitte's pedantic proposals and Raymond Unwin's precise ones represented more of an attempt at resistance or conciliation than a manifestation of acceptance of the inflexible rationalizing will of zoning espoused by engineers and legal experts.

To square the circle, it was necessary to break with the old conventions, something that only the modern movement was capable of. Its unquestionable dogma, that form follows function, was exactly the response that the zoning-based urban planning and the ideology of the "city-machine-commodity" were waiting for.

At this point, we could discuss the circumstances, modes, and consequences of this meeting at greater length, but this would take us far away from our central topic. Therefore, I propose to leave the discussion of the more subterranean layers of our recent past here, in the hope that this preliminary sketch of the matter might be taken up on some other occasion.

Before going any further, however, I would like to add two considerations that I feel are necessary.

The first is that while zoning served conservative goals (its central aim being that of strengthening the power of institutions through the organization of physical space), at least some, if not all, the currents of the modern movement pursued goals of social renewal.

The second is that the consonance between the modern movement and zoning arose from a misunderstanding concerning the principle of "clarity."

While zoning was unquestionably "clear" in character, for the modern movement, "clarity" constituted not only a basis for the refoundation of architectural language but also the measuring stick of architecture's moral integrity: its ultimate teleological goal. The "clear" organization of urban functions proposed by zoning became a solid support for the "clear" organization of urban forms. Then, once the distance between functions and forms was bridged, the path could be traveled in the opposite direction, from forms to functions, and the aesthetic balance of the physical environment could also produce balance in the social environment.

This was the naïve and generous hope of our predecessors, who had understood many things save one: that the relationships between social groups and their physical environment do not unfold according to linear biunivocal processes, and that any attempt to freeze these relationships within simple systems ends up benefitting the few who control the institutions and disadvantaging the many who have no control over them whatsoever. Thus, the faith in "clarity" led the modern movement to make the same mistakes as those of ergonomics and psychoanalysis.

The fact is that "clarity" is not in itself a virtue, nor does it have any exorcising capacity with regard to the content it expresses. There is nothing clearer than an assembly line, a police order, or a declaration of war. Yet "clarity" in no way changes the respectively alienating, repressive, and exterminatory nature of these three events.

On the other hand, "clarity" is not only a legitimate but also an essential goal for language, it being a system of signs intended to make communication possible.

But why should this be the goal of urban organization, which constitutes an infinitely intricate and complex system of relations between individuals and social classes? Why should it be so when the entire system of relations between humans and the physical environment is today characterized by profound contradictions and acute conflicts?

In a situation like this, "clarity" is possible only if it is imposed. One would then have to believe that contradictions and conflicts are the pathological manifestation of maladjusted individuals and social classes, who need to be reeducated or forced to respect institutions, which are by definition wise, just, and healthy. Today, this is hard to believe. In the mid-nineteenth century, Baron Haussmann may have believed it when, in illustrating his plans for the renovation of Paris to Napoleon III, he showed him how the "clear" outline of the grand boulevards made it easy to deploy cannons against rioters if they dared to attack the nerve center of the government. Perhaps, some pioneers of the modern movement believed it too, when in the 1920s they launched the slogan "architecture or revolution."

However, we should not forget that our predecessors were very naïve from a political point of view. It would be fairer to say that they loved their new architectural language so much that they recommended it to the powerful as a means of defending their power. However, it might also be the case that, as often happens with enthusiasts, concealed behind their naïve demeanor was a cunning strategy. If forms follow functions, can it not also be that functions follow forms which, by modifying human behavior, are able to change society? If the powerful had accepted the new architectural language, forms would have started working on their own accord and power would have been eroded.

To avoid being misunderstood, I must say at this point that I too believe that forms can modify human behavior, and that in certain circumstances, forms have the potential to provide imaginaries that help change society. However, I think that this process is not linear but networked; that forms act on human behavior only through feedback; that these feedback loops emerge and produce positive interferences only when forms maintain a continuous relationship with the context that generates them; that the context is the entire system of social forces, with its conflicts and contradictions, and not only the system of institutional forces; that today the social fabric of this context is largely made up by the great masses that are excluded from the Institutions.

But to conclude with the issue of "clarity," which seems to me the origin of the modern movement's misinterpretation of the relationship between form and context, I would like to touch briefly on the problem of housing.

Who does not remember the famous Frankfurt kitchen? At the 1928 CIAM congress in Frankfurt, a kitchen was presented that was so well sized and equipped that a woman could cook an omelet in it with the minimum number of gestures.

The event exemplified an attitude that would have important consequences. Indeed, many other architects of the modern movement would later design other living spaces with the same criteria—bathrooms, bedrooms, living, and dining rooms—and then, again following the same criteria, they would design entire dwellings, entire buildings and finally entire neighborhoods. The procedure was always the same: analyzing all the actions that can occur in the performance of a given function; eliminating all the actions that are considered superfluous; sizing the physical space in which the function is to take place so that it is strictly commensurate with the actions that are deemed necessary and hence not discardable.

Significant contributions have emerged from the application of this method. For the first time, the study of housing was approached with a scientific method, clearing the field of all its accumulated metaphysical stratifications. We should not hesitate to recognize that, without those contributions, we would not have the rich typological vocabulary that still constitutes the premise of accurate design and rational building today. However, having acknowledged it, it is worth taking a deeper look at why those contributions produced such poor results and why all too often those results were so different from the intended outcome.

As I interpret it, Jim Richards has argued that expectations have been diverted by the increasing emphasis on the formal rather than global aspects of the issue. I believe he is right. But the question is, why has the emphasis been placed on the formal rather than the global aspects of the issue? Were there already some conceptual and operational lacunae in the method adopted that were bound to favor such a deviation?

Let us return to the example of the Frankfurt kitchen and try to piece together a few observations.

First of all, it can be said that to select human behaviors one must resort to their "typification," that is, one must imagine a "person type" who produces actions that can be regarded as "typical." We observe that this "person type" has neither society nor history: Their perimeter does not go beyond the rotation span of their limbs. Their behaviors are abstract descriptions that have nothing to do with reality: They are affected neither by contradictions nor conflicts, because the sphere within which the behaviors of the "person type" occur is empty. In scientific research, it is entirely legitimate to use the image of the "typical person" and "typical behavior," as long as it is clear, and explicitly stated when dealing with the results, that these abstract images only provide a first approximation of a much more complex reality.

It can be said then that to judge the degree of usefulness, or uselessness, of a behavior, it is necessary to refer to a scale of values. We observe that the "typical person" has no experience and hence no values nor any capacity for judgment. While this is no doubt obvious to most, what is less obvious is that not only is judgment the absolute prerogative of those who define the "typical person," but it is also already included in the definition itself. What I mean by this is that if the "typical person" is defined, for example, as a human individual whose supreme concern is to cook omelets quickly, any gesture or feeling that hinders this action is to be considered useless and even harmful. Again, from the point of view of scientific research, there is nothing wrong with this definition, provided that it does not become so abstract as to be irrelevant; or, provided that one does not end up applying this definition to certain classes and social groups who, by virtue of being excluded from the decision-making process, seem to live in an empty sphere much like that of the "typical person."

It could also be said that when faced with the task of solving a complex problem, it is correct to reduce the variables to a minimum, as long as one is aware that this is an instrumental operation; in other words, as long as once the values of the variables under consideration have been found, the variables that were provisionally assumed to be constant are reintroduced into the system. If this does not happen, either the result will fail to solve the problem, or the problem will no longer be the one that was initially addressed. In the case of the Frankfurt kitchen, we observe that, once the values of the variables related to cooking omelets have been discovered, the other variables need to be reintroduced as part of the function of a "space used to cook food"; otherwise, the problem that has been solved is merely that of "designing a kitchen so that an omelet can be cooked in it as quickly as possible." The subject is no longer the person who uses the kitchen but the omelet. We are faced with a typical reversal of subject and object.

At this point many more claims could be made, and other inferences drawn, but the central contours of the matter have, perhaps, already been sufficiently outlined. What was said about urban planning can, as was just discussed, also be said about housing.

If we were to turn to the main collective services—schools, hospitals, theaters, shopping centers, traffic systems, and so on—we would, I believe, find the same confluence of aims, motivations, strategies, and tactics that have served as weapons in the process of specialization.

The modern movement appropriated that weaponry and could not escape the dangers that came with it.

At this point, some might wonder why I have characterized specialization, at least twice, as a phenomenon of dangerous degeneration; in short, they might wonder what I actually mean when I say I am against specialization.

I should therefore clarify that I am not against the idea that a particular field of activity should be delimited in as narrow and specific a way as possible in order that it can be explored and experienced with maximum intensity. I am circumspect of indulging in "universal" visions that always turn out to be—especially in architecture—verbose and superficial. On the contrary, I believe that an activity such as ours (like many other intellectual and manual activities) requires an exclusive and continuous commitment that lasts a lifetime. This seems to me to have been the fate of some of the actors who played a key role in the evolution of architecture, as perhaps it has been the fate of all those who, in every activity, intellectual or manual, have devoted all their energy to understanding more deeply the field in which they work, and to enriching it with knowledge and invention.

However, I am against specialization when it becomes a condition of mental segregation that inhibits the critical faculties of those who practice it; in other words, when it severs the relationships between one's field of activity and the outside world, meaning that the purpose of the work becomes the work itself.

Specialization, in the negative sense I ascribe to it, has always existed. In antiquity, the peasants worked the land and did only that for their entire lives; the same could be said for the artisans and the merchants, as well as for those who did not work at all, and who spent their entire lives ordering others around. However, such fields of specialization were more complex and within each there existed pockets of autonomy which left room for a certain range of variations and creative inputs. Everything changed with industrialization when specialization became not just a means of rationalizing production but also a tool of social control. Under such conditions, specialization meant not simply focusing on a field of activity to competently carry out a set of prescribed and generally repetitive operations but having no care for the broader motivations and consequences of these operations. If the result was higher productivity, and sometimes a higher salary, this was paid for with the renunciation of criticism and dissent. Institutions, governed by individuals specialized exclusively in running Institutions, acquired the prerogative of developing a global vision, while those working within their field, and within the limits set by their specialization, were granted the freedom to move only within their own spheres, with each sphere enabling only partial visions. The diameter of these spheres is larger or smaller according to the "institutional" importance of the activities that they encompass. The sphere of the scientists is larger than that of the technicians, which is larger than that of the professionals, which is larger than that of the artists, all the way down to the sphere of the assembly line workers, which is larger than that of the cotton-pickers, and so on and so forth. This hierarchical sequence can also be manipulated if circumstances arise when Institutions need to be protected, strengthened, or adorned. Then, it may happen that the military sphere becomes the largest, or that of the astronauts, or abstract painters, or even that of a certain group of workers digging a dangerous tunnel under a towering mountain.

In such cases, the size of the sphere is more illusory than real, in that its proportions have been artificially dilated through rhetoric; but the substance of the phenomenon does not change. As long as individuals do not cast their eyes beyond their own sphere, everyone who specializes receives some kind of reward, more or less important depending on the scales of values and "institutional" circumstances.

In describing these as spheres, I have used an abstract spatial geometrical term. I have done so to pursue a metaphor, but I think it is not difficult to move from this abstract image to the real object that is the central topic of our discussion, namely physical space. For, at a certain point, physical space began to be implicated in the development of specialization; that is, at a certain point in recent history, it was discovered that the specialization of physical space could be instrumental in perfecting the specialization of human activities. From that moment onward, not only those individuals who worked within the spheres but the spheres themselves began to be internally unified.

Let us consider what had occurred before this discovery. While peasants specialized in peasant labor, within the limits of their productive activity, they had a sufficient degree of freedom to creatively express their needs and to choose the most appropriate ways to represent themselves and their relations with society and nature. The same was true for citizens, whether they were artisans, merchants, students, clergymen, or wealthy landowners. The houses and farming hamlets scattered across the countryside each had a specific structure and formal layout so rich in connotations as to constitute a narrative event, giving expression to the aspirations, sorrows, struggles, and hopes of their inhabitants. The same was true of the cities and each of their districts.

What happened when the principle of specialization was extended to the organization of the physical environment? As a result, everything became flat and anonymous; as in the workplace, the possibility of self-expression and self-representation was lost in all activities of life. One might say that this was bound to happen as a natural consequence of demographic expansion, increased mobility and the interpenetration of local cultures. There is probably some truth to it, but what is interesting to note is that the specialization of physical space had two fundamental effects (or two fundamental motivations, depending on one's view of the phenomenon; that is, depending on whether one considers it as occurring naturally or deliberately). The first "effect-motivation" was the subjugation of physical space to the needs of production and, hence, to the power of those who govern production processes. The second "effect-motivation" was the use of physical space as an instrument for the control and repression of social life. The two effects (or motivations) led to the organization of physical space exercising the same function already performed by the division of labor: that of accelerating and institutionalizing the fragmentation of human life.

I believe that this account implicitly answers the questions I posed earlier, but I shall now try to address them more directly.

Why have the contributions of the modern movement been so scarce? Because the scientific content that informed the first approaches to the problem of organizing physical space rapidly lost its way in the labyrinths of schematization and became trapped in models that gave the illusion of grasping reality while, in truth, they profoundly altered it.

Why did the contributions of the modern movement yield results so different from what was expected? Because the problem of organizing physical space had been approached with the same criteria that are adopted when organizing the production of a commodity. Thus, the proposed solutions proved to be more comprehensible and utilizable to those who benefit from the commodification of human activity and thought, rather than those who are oppressed by it.

Why did the modern movement ended up placing more emphasis on the formal rather than the global aspects of the issue? Because the modern movement lost touch with and even awareness of the context in which it needed (and wanted) to operate.

The form-function equation, however debatable it may seem today, could have yielded far more than it has if its second term had not been limited to a poor representation of conventional behaviors but, on the contrary, had been stretched to encompass the whole range of social behaviors and all the contradictions and conflicts that characterize them.

But this understanding would have required the direct participation of the primary users, whereas the method adopted required that they be excluded and their voices unheard. The loss of contextual awareness first altered and then emptied of meaning the set of propositions that the modern movement had initially pursued. There was no other path left than to take refuge in the heated arrogance of art or the cold neutrality of technique, to indulge in the excitement of aesthetic research or the calm detachment of professional practice.

It seems to me that these responses contain, together with the criticism of what has happened to architecture in the past few years, an indication of what could happen in the future. What seems certain to me is that today we find ourselves at a crossroads and that each of the two directions will be decisive not only for architecture, but also for the evolution of the relationship between physical space and society.

It seems clear that, except for a few pockets that have not yet been attacked, people's ability to control their environment is about to be removed even further from political debate and overridden by the obscure and automated logic of power. Environmental transformations follow this logic and assume the structures most appropriate to producing the symbols through which power is expressed. It is enough to mention here the example of the automobile, which as a means of urban transport no longer makes sense and yet continues to be a decisive factor in determining the location of activities and their spatial configurations.

There are no technical or even economic obstacles (especially if social costs are considered) to prevent us from replacing urban car transport with high-tech, high-speed, quiet, and comfortable public transport systems. But this is not happening, and probably will not happen for a long time, not so much because the operation does not suit the automobile industry or the big oil companies, but because the car has become by now more of a symbol (charged with almost perfect ambiguity) than a means of transport. Its symbolic power lies in its ability to generate the illusion that power is widespread and within everyone's reach, while in fact—precisely by virtue of this illusion—power concentrates and strengthens its hold not only in the economic sector but also in human communication.

The myth of the automobile provides a striking example of how physical space can be manipulated to bring about a state of total alienation that guarantees social stability. However, by examining current trends, we could find many other cases, perhaps less obvious but also more insidious. For instance, the myth of the suburb in the United States, or the myth of the historic center in Europe, as well as the myths of the model towns, of urban renewal and beautification programs.

To this latter family belongs the supreme myth according to which certain "nodes" of intense architectural quality can counterbalance the squalor of the urban fabric they are placed within. This scheme is starting to garner success—especially in the capital cities of large metropolitan areas—due to its ability to materialize symbols that are ideologically ambiguous. These nodes of intense architectural quality (which generally coincide with the sites where politics, bureaucracy, finance, and the mainstream media are entrenched) are offered and welcomed as expressions of the entire community, while in fact they foster the fragmentation of social groups by alienating them from the concrete problems of the physical space in which they actually live.

For this reason, I must confess that I find myself unable to share Jim Richards's suggestive "two architectures" hypothesis. While I recognize the merit of his attempt to realistically account for an ongoing trend,

I would hesitate to recognize as realistic his assumption that this trend evolves according to a logic that is not its own. For the development of nodes of intense architectural quality is intended to cover up the lack of quality of the surrounding urban fabric and to divert attention from the strictly quantitative robberies being carried out on it.

It seems unlikely that this trend would undergo a spontaneous change of direction, and even more unlikely that such change would be triggered by the pressure of an advanced construction technology which, to be honest, does not yet exist.

But I have another, perhaps more profound, reason for not being able to accept the "two architectures" hypothesis. I do not believe that progress can be used to justify technique, nor the alleviation of human anguish to justify art, and much less technique and art to justify architecture. In other words, I do not think that a new technical discovery that does not improve the material conditions of humankind can be considered acceptable, even if it advances technique; nor a new artistic invention that does not increase the critical imagination of humankind, even if it succeeds in alleviating feelings of anguish through the magic of illusions; nor a new architectural event that does not counter the fragmentation of human life, even if it is technically irreproachable and artistically evocative.

On the other hand, it does not seem important to me at this point in time to provide architecture with a route to escape the grip of its age-old dilemma—between technique and art—by guaranteeing it the tranquility of a dual existence along its technical and artistic axes. Nor does it seem important to me to guarantee a legitimate role for architects by offering them a choice between one existence or the other.

The prospect that I actually find most interesting is that of taking architecture away from architects and giving it back to the people who use it.

I do not want to sound arrogant toward my fellow architects (and hence toward myself), so I would like to add straight away that I consider the contribution that architects can make to the achievement of this goal to be of great importance. This is, in fact, the crossroads at which architecture finds itself today, and it is largely down to architects whether the road taken will be the right one.

A crossroads, by definition, has two branches. In our case, one of the two branches is an extension of the road architecture has traveled so far; the other branch, by contrast, splinters off in a new direction. This new direction leads toward an architecture of participation.

At this point, I should probably try to define what an architecture of participation is and to give some indication of how it can be practiced.

This is certainly no easy task, since the architecture of participation does not yet exist, nor does any authentic form of participation, at least in that part of the world that we call "civilized."

Participation occurs only when all are equally involved in the administration of power, or—to make it clearer—when power no longer exists because all are directly and equally involved in decision-making processes.

I imagine the first objection will be that I am describing a utopia. This is a fair objection because the architecture of participation is indeed a utopia; however, it is a realistic one, which makes all the difference.

In its common understanding, utopia presents an impossible image, because it involves a complete alteration of the context to which it is opposed, meaning that it does not take into account the variables that constitute reality. If, by contrast, we consider all of these variables and assume that the relations that constitute them could be different—because they could well be—then utopia becomes realistic. In our case, the context consists of forces that have been expressed through violence and forces that have been exalted through the same violence; hence, the system of relations between these forces is artificial. Indeed, it is artificial to have a situation in which only the will of bureaucracy, politics, finance, the mainstream media, and so forth, plays a decisive role in the organization of physical space, while the will of the poor and disenfranchised (who make up the majority of the population) counts for nothing. If a counterimage for organizing physical space does not omit any of the forces acting in the context and takes into account not only their actual but also their potential energies, and thereby disrupts the image derived from the present artificial situation, then the counterimage presents a realistic utopia. It is a utopia that will become actual when the latent energies have all been released to subvert the conditions of oppression that currently stifle them.

Although we find ourselves in a different context of ideas, we are not far off from Le Corbusier's statement that "utopia is the reality of tomorrow," to quote a "predecessor" who I profoundly admire precisely because of his ability to break with conformism even when passed off as serious realism.

I imagine that, perhaps prompted by this invocation, another reasonable objection may arise. The equilibrium of forces that constitute the present context may be artificial, but it is stable and does not seem close to breaking down: If architecture does not accept this condition, then what is to be done about it?

Here I believe we need to articulate a response that takes as its starting point at least two premises. First, I maintain that an architectural image can have significant effects even if it does not become actual (as long as it is so charged with potential energy that it seriously undermines the forces that oppose its realization). It can debunk the most deeply rooted clichés, reveal the stupidity or injustice of passively accepted situations, awaken an awareness of rights that one does not dare claim, outline a hitherto unknown destination that from that moment on becomes a target to aim for.

From the second half of the nineteenth century to the early years of the twentieth century, a series of images were produced that did not achieve immediate success and yet not only did they shake up thinking about architecture and urban planning; they also contributed to changing the political and social perspectives of their contemporaries and the generations that followed. We could recall here figures such as Robert Owen, Victor Considerant, Benjamin Richardson, William Morris, Piotr Kropotkin, Patrick Geddes, and—why not?—Mr. Paxton and Mr. Eiffel, and then Louis Henry Sullivan, Adolf Loos, and Le Corbusier, for their many contradictory contributions.

I mention only these characters, and not others, intentionally (even though the list of the official critics is much longer) to make it clear that I am not talking about "fairy tales." For I do not believe in heroes who ride along the paths of Wonderland for the sake of intellectual adventure, but I do believe in counterheroes who spend all their energy, engage their cunning, and risk their candor to construct images that seek to bring about concrete and possible alternatives to the present world. What seems important to me is this: If the most authentic forces of the present context were to break the artificial state of equilibrium in which they are imprisoned, those images would become actual; but it is the fact that those images have the possibility of becoming actual that sets the context in motion and helps to break its artificial state of equilibrium.

The second premise is that systems are never perfect. Even the smoothest and most compact systems are furrowed by a network of deep fissures caused by their internal contradictions. Hence, it is always possible, when traversing this network, to find cracks where innovative events can be inserted; events that, once introduced, grow and widen the cracks, or produce others, and thus contribute to making manifest that the logic of the system cannot hold and must be replaced with another less contradictory one. Innovative events are certainly not consistent with the structure of the system, but often (and it does not matter how often) the system fails to reject them.

Among the many possible cases we could examine to test this claim, let us take the case of communication, which is not only highly consequential but also concerns us directly. All the systems—at least in the so-called civilized world—are making great efforts to secure absolute dominance over the field of human communication.

This objective is seductive—after all, it has held sway in the imagination of the powerful in every age—because, after achieving dominance over communication, social control would become absolute, and much more meticulous than that exercised through the control of economic resources. That is why systems invest huge amounts of material and intellectual means to develop devices designed to transmit, receive, and record all kinds of information. But to be widely disseminated, the devices must be simple, miniaturized, and cheaply produced. Herein lies the contradiction: Since they are easy to handle, compact, and inexpensive, communication devices are also within everyone's reach. The system produces instruments of control designed to increase its power, but at the same time it is forced to make these means available to those who wish to defend their independence against the expansion of power.

I am speaking not of science fiction but of real facts that are already taking place. I am referring, just to give an example, to initiatives such as that of radical software, which, by putting together all the devices owned by its young members, builds extensive communication networks to broadcast clandestine news programs that contradict the coverage provided by mainstream channels in the United States.

Moreover, similar phenomena, albeit obviously different in character, are also occurring in the organization of physical space. There is no longer a corner of the urbanized territories where the capillary expansion of institutional control is not attempted, but the reach of such interventions has become so wide as to no longer afford any real form of control. It is necessary for its actions to be sweeping, swift, and brutal. Whenever a motorway needs to be laid out, a nature park destroyed, or a neighborhood gutted, whenever a new business center or industrial area are to be built, or an historic center embalmed, and so on, not only are the inhabitants left uninformed but the ecological, technological, economic, and sociological consequences of the intervention undertaken are not even properly assessed. When building a housing estate, an industrial plant, or an office center, not only are the needs of the people who live and work there disregarded, it is not even possible to establish the threshold beyond which the failure to satisfy such needs undermines the more immediate goals of the initiative.

As it is extended, this system of control is revealed to be increasingly incompetent and stupid, hence, breeding revolt. In recent years, we have witnessed explosions of refusal that were never imagined possible. The initial spark came from university students, but this phenomenon has since spread and taken root in all the social strata who have better reasons than university students for not accepting current societal conditions. If the targets of refusal were at first particular and limited, they now tend be global in their focus, spreading to the whole system of values imposed by the Institutions.

Once again, the problem of "why" starts to take precedence over the problem of "how." In such moments, the absurdity of many situations that had hitherto been taken for granted becomes evident.

We begin to discover that the fragmentation of human life destroys the integrity of individuals and isolates them from society depriving them of any capacity to defend themselves; that work should not be the ultimate purpose but only a means to improve one's existence and to communicate with others; that specialization is an alienating practice if it only serves to increase production and profit and not to enhance the creative potential of the workers.

In the domain of physical space, there is a growing awareness that any intervention in the city or the territory is determined either by the greed of real estate developers or the obtusity of bureaucrats. That is why it is difficult to keep faith in surveys, programs, plans, interdisciplinary teams, social scientists, urban planners, and architects—all the agents that combine to produce incomprehensible events, which always have the same aims and lead to the same conclusions.

As for those of us who have also been hit by the surging wave of refusal, we are beginning to suspect that our role is not only precarious but also ambiguous and that perhaps we need to revise the way we practice architecture to restore legitimacy to both ourselves and architecture.

Can we then say that we are ready to change direction? Perhaps we can only say that a new direction has revealed itself and that it represents a concrete alternative to the present.

I think I have reached the last amongst the points I set out to discuss: What changes in architecture if we move from its traditional authoritarian way of operating to a new practice based on participation?

I will now try to conclude the issue by adding just a few notes that might shed some additional light on the most important points. In truth, I do not intend to say much because I do not think it possible: After all, the practice of participation should be developed and fine-tuned through participation.

Note 1. Project and Process

An architectural operation passes through three moments: the definition of a problem, the elaboration of a solution, and the evaluation of the results. The sequence of these three moments is irreversible, and by the end of its course the operation is considered complete. Each moment is separate from the others: Each influences the next moment only accidentally and does not exert any retroactive feedback on the previous moment. Only the central moment is considered truly relevant. The first serves to gather evidence to justify the second, while the third is practically nonexistent.

The procedures used in the first moment—that of problem definition—are inaccurate and unsystematic. Often one resorts to intuition and just as often to extensive compilations of data. Yet, both the intuitive and the compilatory approach are often distorted by the values of those who carry out the investigation, who are typically the same people who also elaborate the project. The objectives are taken for granted: The global aims are not discussed but only the immediate repercussions that affect the cost, economics, technique, and aesthetics of the project. The resources allocated to the operation are taken as a given, even when (as in the case of low-cost housing) they are distributed in such a way as to create inequalities in standards and, hence, segregation. The will of the recipients is either ignored as a matter of principle or counterfeited through the application of models that fit the interests of those who sponsor the operation or the visions of those who design it.

The moment of elaborating a solution goes from the design of the project to its execution. The design tends to consist of a unique object that admits no alternatives. It may happen that, before being realized, the object undergoes some adjustments or that, at most, it is rejected and then replaced with a more appropriate one. But when this happens, the dispute occurs only between the client and the designer, and the object of dispute is almost always financial. Once accepted, the project is executed and, once executed, is handed over to the user. Use has no influence over the object produced; on the contrary, the object is considered all the more successful the more it can resist the subversions of use.

The moment of evaluating the results is, as I have already said, practically irrelevant, and could not be otherwise for two reasons. The first is the tendency to consider the architectural product as a work of art, hence, as a unique event, which by definition is irreducible to any kind of rational comparison. The second is that the falsification of objectives and the disregard for use make it impossible to establish any criteria of judgment that would allow a comparison between the intended outcome and what is actually achieved. For this reason, each new architectural episode has no precedents (except aesthetic or financial) and does not constitute a precedent (except aesthetic or financial) for other subsequent episodes: it is an isolated case that does not fit within a larger process.

So far I have described what happens in the practice of authoritarian design. But what happens instead if the design practice is based on participation?

Participation implies the presence of users throughout the whole operation. This fact has at least three fundamental consequences: Each moment of the operation becomes a phase of the project; even "use" becomes a moment of the operation and thus a phase of the project; the different moments merge with each other, and the operation ceases to be linear, one-way, and self-sufficient.

Here I feel it is important to be clear, so I shall add a few brief explanations.

The moment of defining problems is part of the project in the sense that the objectives of the operation and the resources allocated to it are bound to become the subject of discussion with future users. (A program for building a subsidized residential district may be internally coherent and yet wrong with regard to the makeup of the area in which it is located; the resources allocated to the program may be proportionate to the financial logic of the operation and yet insufficient to meet the most legitimate expectations. Only a discussion with the users can bring out these contradictions and resolve them; or if not resolve them, it can at least make them explode into an open conflict.)

The moment of elaborating solutions no longer tends toward a single, finished product, but toward a sequence of hypotheses that continue to be refined as users respond to them with criticism and creative contributions. (The task of the designer is no longer that of churning out finished and unalterable solutions, but to extract solutions from an ongoing confrontation with those who will use their work. Their imagination will be entirely aimed at awakening the imagination of their interlocutors, and the solution will emerge from the contact between the two, passing through a concatenation of alternatives, which become progressively more appropriate to the nature of the problem addressed).

The verification of the results refers to the way in which the product is used, and the judgment will be more or less positive depending on whether the needs of users have been more or less met. (These are not only practical needs but also creative needs. In addition to improving the material conditions of its recipients, a work of architecture must also support their communicational needs by representing them. For this reason, the structure of the work must be conceived in such a way as to allow for continuous adaptations and new transformations, which can be substantiated as true extensions of the project.)

Thereby, the practice of participation changes every moment of the architectural operation as well as the system of relations between the different moments. Each moment acts on those that follow it and retroactively affects those that precede it, until the set of actions and retroactions overrides the operation which contains it and is projected outward onto other similar operations. Through this process of mutual transformation, objectives, solutions, modes of use, and criteria of judgment generate an experience that continues to grow. (Architectural design becomes a process.)

Note 2. Order and Disorder

It seems interesting to me that some influential contemporary architects have claimed Las Vegas to be one of the most beautiful cities in the world[1]; and it seems equally interesting to me that pop art has found in the most trivial objects of our time a vital material worthy of artistic representation. I believe that both these facts have broadened the spectrum of human communication because they have introduced into common use some forms of expression that had hitherto been considered irrelevant or even execrable. However, I do not believe that the consequences have been as subversive and unequivocal as many critics claim.

After all, the discovery of Las Vegas represents mainly a declaration of independence toward the abstract technocratic fanaticism of the followers of Mies van der Rohe and toward the tedious moralistic admonitions of the Bauhaus epigones.

The discovery of triviality, on the other hand, represents mainly a final irreverent shakeup of the old principle according to which Art is the representation of Beauty.

In fact, however, the two discoveries were "internal disputes" within the domains of Architecture and Art and outside these domains they did not really frighten anyone: If anything, they contributed to making certain embarrassing anomalies in economic and social development more acceptable.

Fifty years earlier, the Dada movement went down the same path but explored it with a different rigor that went to the heart of the problem: that a state of "order" occurs when a set of things or ideas takes on a configuration consistent with the system of values imposed by the official Institutions, and that one breaks free from this imposition by opposing "order" with the creative energies of "disorder."

Architecture is by definition an activity that "brings order." From Vitruvius to the present day, there has not been a treatise, program, or project that has not reconfirmed this role for architecture. Yet it is easy for anyone to ascertain that a physical system is all the more vital the more information is required to describe it, that is, the higher its level of entropy, or the more advanced its state of disorder. Perhaps even Vitruvius (like Peter Blake and almost all of us), when visiting a city, quickly tired of admiring the grand avenues of order and ducked instead into the alleys of disorder, where activities swarm, organizational systems intertwine, and forms flourish. The truth is that in order there is the frustrating boredom of imposition, while in disorder there is the exhilarating creativity of participation.

Note 2 could end here, since its function is not to solve a problem but to outline it. However, having started with the example of Las Vegas, I feel it necessary to add three brief observations so as not to be misunderstood.

The first is that there are two types of disorder in physical space. The first arises from situations of independence from or insubordination to the flattening processes produced by institutional control and manifests itself where the free expression of the community is still possible. The second arises from pathological situations of institutional control and manifests itself where, in the absence of opposition, control produces anomalies that overwhelm its own rules. The first type of disorder is that of participation; the second is that of alienation, exploitation, and violence.

The second observation is that the "disorder" of participation is not an unstructured and accidental phenomenon. On the contrary, it is founded on systems of values and modes of behavior that are far more articulate and flexible than those on which order is founded. Architecture has rarely produced complex events because, clouded by its vocation for order, it has failed to penetrate the logic of disorder. Even when it has been intensely preoccupied with people, its aim was to convert them to a system based on order.

The third observation is to note that disorder, unlike order, cannot be planned. Those who have attempted to do so have designed a disordered order that is still a form of order. For the real question is not to reproduce the external aspects of disorder but establishing the conditions under which disorder can freely manifest itself.

Note 3. Open Systems

Over the past fifteen years, certain architectural currents have been involved in the search for open systems. Open systems are flexible, mutable, growing projects that can be implemented in phases. If at the end of each phase the systems assume a finite configuration, albeit one that can readily be reopened, then they are called "open-ended systems."

There are diverse and concomitant reasons behind the search for open systems. There are sociological reasons stemming from the realization that the variability of individual and social behavior is becoming ever more dynamic. Therefore, it seems unreasonable that any set of activities should be enclosed in an inflexible and finite physical structure. For either the structure would prevent the development of activities, or the development of activities would destroy the structure.

There are also economic reasons stemming from the realization that the gap between the functional and physical obsolescence of a structure is becoming wider—in other words, that the period of fully utilizing a structure is becoming shorter and shorter in relation to its lifespan, which remains more or less constant. This then leads to waste that could be avoided by using structures that are either more rapidly consumed or capable of adapting themselves to changes in the activities they contain. There are also technological reasons stemming from the realization that the development of technology is making more fluid the relationships between the various elements that comprise a structure. Therefore, attention must now focus more on the quality of the connections through which such relationships are established (software) rather than on the material quality of the set of elements (hardware).

Finally, there are many other complementary reasons that refer to the organization and quality of forms, to their capacity to signify and communicate vis-à-vis a society that tends to replace the tranquility of contemplation with the stimuli of increasingly intense emotional solicitations. Guided by these various reasons, research on open systems has yielded very interesting results. The most significant works produced in recent years come out of this matrix. It is interesting to note that—even though this was not always clear to its promoters—research on open systems has made an important contribution to the formation of an architecture based on participation. On the one hand, it challenged all principles of purity, autonomy, self-sufficiency, which made architecture impenetrable to its public. On the other hand, it paved the way for the transformation of design into a process by reaffirming the existence of a mutually necessary relationship between the way the environment is organized and the continuous evolution of the context for which the environment is organized.

Note 4. Architecture Is Dead, Long Live Architecture!

If we were to take a dispassionate look at what is happening today, we could conclude that nobody seems to be interested in architecture anymore. The traditional clients are no longer interested because it does not efficiently and rapidly solve their problems of investment and power; institutions are no longer interested because it produces symbols that are too feeble and faded in comparison to those produced by other, more powerful and aggressive sectors; ordinary people are no longer interested because it does not propose anything that matches their expectations.

Thus, since there is no longer any interest in it, architecture is condemned to rapid extinction. This is not a joke to frighten architects (who will in any case be saved either by adapting to the new situation or by retreating to isolated reserves, where fragments of architectural memory will continue to be artificially cultivated for the curiosity of a few). One need only to scroll through the diagnoses of experts that underpin the decisions of the politicians entrusted with the fate of the world to become convinced that this is neither an incendiary joke nor a facile quip. These diagnoses all concur in declaring that the organization of physical space is a very serious issue but also a very simple one. To solve it, one need only identify the most salient problems—namely residence and transport—and entrust them to those who can deal with them as quickly and with as little effort as possible.

The implementation of this program implies, first of all, recognizing the obstacles to promptly avoid them and then resorting to the most effective tools for what they can deliver, without expecting a qualitative performance that is extraneous to their nature.

For example, the city constitutes an insurmountable obstacle due to its morphological and social complexity: hence, it should be ignored. All efforts should be instead concentrated on the formation of suburbs, located where it is easy to find the necessary areas. The structure of these suburbs can also consist of trailers, or other similar devices that can be quickly, accurately, and cheaply mass-produced. The connections between the suburbs can be ensured through a widespread network of roads that the state bureaucracy will set up expanding the tasks already entrusted to it.

If programs of this kind are implemented, the world will be cleansed of all forms of architecture. But will the world be able to do without architecture? It will if architecture continues to be of no use to anyone. It will not if architecture changes.

If architecture abandons the authoritarian position it holds today, and if it goes over to the side of the people, the people will defend architecture.

I have thus come to the end of my reflections. I realize that I have discussed issues which perhaps do not entirely coincide with those that the organizers of the meetings in Melbourne had asked me to address.

I apologize for this, but I fear that if I had done otherwise, I would have not known what to say. In fact, the premise that guides my current research is that the architecture of the 1970s will be interesting (in the sense that it will become a fundamental topic of cultural and social debate) only if it takes the path that I have tried to describe—that is, if it is characterized by an increasing user participation in its organizational and formal definition; if—with the help of architects—it is less and less the representation of those who design it and more and more the representation of those who use it.

Planning and Participation: The Case of Rimini

I must confess that I am unsure whether today you expect me to speak about the plan for the new center of Rimini or about the theory and methodology of popular participation as it relates to urban planning more generally. If, in other words, I am expected to tackle head-on a still heated situation in which I have been a direct protagonist, or to discuss with relative detachment the experimental research that I have been conducting for some time.

Finding myself faced with this uncertainty—about my choices and your expectations—I suspect that my intervention will end up following a sinusoidal path, touching the edges of both topics without claiming to penetrate them fully. On the one hand, I will talk about the plan for the new center of Rimini by referring to the episodes of popular participation that characterized it, and, on the other, I will make a few observations about the theory and methodology of participation by referring to how these were applied in the plan. In this way

I hope to avoid both being polemical when speaking about the plan and being abstract when speaking about participation.

To begin, it is important to state that defining participation is difficult. Carlo Doglio claimed to be unsure whether the current talk of participation in urban planning represents the beginning or the end of a cycle of experiences. It is an interesting observation: for if it were an end, it would represent corruption and cunning; whereas if it were a beginning, it would represent discovery and hope.

It could be both depending on the circumstances, the forces at play, the promoters, and so on. However, I would like to make a case in favor of the hypothesis that we are at a beginning. For such hypothesis appears plausible to me, if we focus our attention not on the abstract categories of power, but on the concrete reality of an ever-increasing—and indisputable—presence of a will for popular participation.

As is well known, Adenauer—the chancellor of West Germany, who perhaps few among the young people in attendance here remember—was one of the first to talk about participation. He meant participation in corporate profits by means of extending the ownership of company shares to the workers. No doubt this was a ruse to capture the consent of workers by presenting them with the mirage of ownership. It is also certain, however, that this ruse was mirrored in the desire expressed by German workers to reject capitalist subjugation.

Even De Gaulle argued for the need to reorganize production on a new participatory basis, by which he meant something more or less analogous to what Adenauer had meant. Once more, this was a ruse (albeit one more enlightened and thus sustained by sincere and anachronistic paternalistic impulses), and again it found itself mirrored in the French students and workers who had turned France upside down by opening to public use all urban spaces structurally reserved for private institutions.

Is this the same as what is happening in urban planning? Perhaps so, given all the uncertainties and convolutions characteristic of an activity that has hitherto been considered little more than an accessory, and that moreover has up until now been incapable of developing a scientific backbone. Looking only at the last fifty years, we can discern in its course an initial enlightened period in which the mirage of a formal order—as a cover for the unruliness of the system of social and political governance—kindled the minds of the most admirable urban planners as well as the most ignorant. Then came a second period, that of the glorification of development—which in Italy coincided with the first center-left government—in which the sole requirement was the channeling of actions toward goals of maximum efficiency. These goals were to be achieved by resorting to precise techniques of analysis and intervention, the precision of which could be attained at the highest level only by suspending value judgments, which were themselves considered polluting factors. Finally came the third period in which we began to realize that both the mirage of formal order and the neutral glorification of development were rhetorical devices designed to adorn capitalist exploitation and bureaucratic repression, and that, by proceeding along these paths, the reality of urban planning—regardless of its academic abstractions—would start to generate clashes. At this point, it was once again argued that value judgments were the real underlying motivations behind all analyses and interventions, and so we turned—in certain sectors—to discussing participation.

Doglio is justified in asking whether this arrival is the beginning or the end of a cycle, but I think he is mistaken when he seems to suggest that it is an end. We know that much of the current discussion on participation is an attempt at capturing consensus, while continuing to protect exploitation and repression through the cover of a new rhetorical ornamentation. However, there are also popular groups that are taking direct action and affirming with concrete acts their right to shape and manage physical space according to their needs; and there are even some architects and urban planners—only a few to be honest—who are arguing for a refounding of architecture and urban planning, and the redefinition of their own role based on this new reality.

There is some confusion between these two branches: that of participation tamed by power and that of participation manifested through direct action. There is also confusion within this second branch, which I will address later. But it seems to me that the shift that has taken place is equally important as it opens up a new perspective, the materialization of which is no longer entrusted to purely intellectual exercises but to the orientations and outcomes of social dialectics.

It is interesting to note how this is happening simultaneously all over the world, and even in the United States (where, after all, the phenomenon appeared much earlier than elsewhere), with the occurrence of urban uprisings against overpowering territorial interventions decided from above, and with the formation of a dense network of resistance comprising legions of new technicians who put their expertise at the service of communities and against power.

It was in this context that advocacy planning took shape as a form of grassroots intervention into urban planning. The typical scope of such interventions is the neighborhood unit, generally made up of poor and segregated minorities who are assisted by groups of volunteers specialized in various disciplines related to the transformation and management of the territory. It should be said that in recent years advocacy planning has lost its initial energy, being on the one hand coopted by power and on the other tempted by paternalism. However, from its seeds more radical tendencies have blossomed, which increasingly work "with" rather than "for" the community. With even greater clarity of purpose and perhaps more energy, similar transformative actions of urban planning are unfolding in many other countries around the world, such as (to cite two opposite examples) Argentina and England.

In our country—as in others in Western Europe—where there is an idealistic tendency to consider the microcosm as irrelevant, and to think that interventions in the immediate physical surroundings should automatically ensue from a palingenesis that will first transform the entire macrocosm, grassroots interventions into urban planning have struggled to emerge. No technicians could be found who believed in them, nor, quite extraordinarily, could politicians be found who considered them significant. Thus, in our country, grassroots interventions into urban planning arose directly from the base. This base discovered for itself a truth that might seem obvious today but was not a few years ago: The territory is always analyzed, transformed, organized, exploited, and so on, to the advantage of power and therefore to the disadvantage of the working classes.

I just said that this is an obvious truth. To prove it, let us take a case study; and, to keep our promise, let us take the case of the city of Rimini.

Each city contains within its organizational system and formal configuration a precise record of how physical space has been distributed in any period of its existence. For those who know how to read the stratifications of the urban context, it is clear "who" exploited and "when" and "how" such exploitation took place, as well as "who" was exploited and "to what extent," in and through the territory. The signs are always precise and unequivocal, much more so than in written histories.

In Rimini, urban planning events are particularly exemplary: It is enough to compare—through documents, preexisting artifacts, and other sources—the various phases of urban development, and to observe the many urban plans that the city's administrations have had drawn up over the last sixty years (both approved and shelved, the latter often richer in consequences than the former).

Perhaps at some point I will share all the observations on the subject that I had the opportunity to make in Rimini. For now, I shall limit myself to citing a case that to me seems not only exceptionally significant but also very topical. This is the case of the foundation of the seaside district of Marina.

The first bathing establishment in Marina had been built under papal rule. The private decision had not lacked public support: In fact, at the same time as the establishment was being built, the municipality had laid out the long straight stretch of road that is still referred to as the road of the baths in popular parlance. In 1861, the railway station was placed at the junction between the city walls and this stretch of road.

The matrix of a new urban development was thus stamped on the city with perfect accord between private economic power and public administrative power. The premise was the exploitation of the long coastal strip: The bridgehead had already been launched with the first bathing establishment; the road of the baths ensured its connection with the city, whose distribution of interests had been opportunely concealed through the skillful placement of the railway. Now the intention was to begin expanding Marina, and it was necessary to do so prudently, hiding the objective of exploitation behind false goals. In 1873, a short distance to the south of the bathing establishment, a hydrotherapy resort was founded for children suffering from scrofula, which enabled them to enjoy the sea. But so that the resort did not remain isolated, a savings bank and a limited constructions company began to parcel out and build detached houses on the area separating it from the bathing establishment. On the other hand, the resort had to be accessible, so the municipality laid out the first tramway for horsecars connecting the station with the coast and continuing beyond the resort.

At this point, recognizing that the area had one of the best developed infrastructures in Rimini, the municipality claimed that there was a risk of speculation and declared it state property. Now, all was well: People were happy since they had proof that this was a social operation. Except that in 1906, when the infrastructure had been perfected with further developments to the railway, the small interests were hijacked, the limited construction company reaped its profits, the state property freeze was suddenly lifted, and the path was paved for indiscriminate exploitation of the land. As for the hydrotherapy resort, it was judged inadequate for the social level of the area and the children suffering from scrofula were sent home.

The foundation of Marina and the direction taken by its expansion have had a profound impact on all aspects of Rimini's development. It has impacted not only the urban layout (which today is distorted by profound organizational and morphological imbalances), and the economic structure (which has become monofunctional and therefore lacks the possibility of diversification and internal rebalancing), but also the social configuration, which tends to be uniform and middle-class, especially in urban areas. Proletarian culture and consciousness, so pronounced at the time of the Red Week, seem to survive only in certain areas: in San Giuliano, in a few subsidized ghettos in the northern suburbs and in some rural hamlets.[1]

But the point I would like to make and discuss now is that the development of Marina took place unbeknownst to the popular classes. The crude but tenacious entanglement of economic and political-administrative power, embellished with the rhetoric of progress, sought to pass off as a patriotic action what was a speculative operation that advantaged only a few financiers and entrepreneurs and disadvantaged many fishermen, sailors, porters, artisans, and peasants. Sixty years later, these operations have become unconscious—like a habit we no longer pay attention to—but they continue to move ahead; and while some disadvantaged groups have faded away, others have been added. The latter include seasonal or day laborers recruited in the countryside or other more depressed regions with no guarantee of wages or welfare, but also the smallest landlords condemned to a desperate existence amidst unpaid bills and the extorsions of tourist agencies.

The development of Marina in Rimini is thus an example of how a minority can exploit a territory to the detriment of the majority, and also of how urban planning can play a role in covering up such exploitation by passing off as progressive interventions that would turn out to be fraught with substantially negative consequences. It follows that urban planning—despite being a superstructural activity—has the capacity to produce material determinations that impact on the economic structure, and that this capacity can be expressed (or "must" be, if it is to assume political legitimacy) firstly by involving the popular classes in the motivations and consequences of its interventions, and secondly by taking their side in the inevitable conflict between class interests unleashed by such interventions.

It is, in essence, a matter of 'taking a side'—this is the frontier at which urban planning finds itself. But "taking a side" does not mean acting with the good intention of protecting and defending the side one has chosen, let alone seeking to obtain consensus. For to do so would not in fact deviate much from the objectives of the astute Adenauer or the paternalistic De Gaulle. To "take a side" means giving that "side" the leading role and profoundly transforming the function of the urban planner. In such a situation, the function of the urban planner would no longer be to receive from power a description of the problem and solve it according to the instructions given; nor to identify, describe, and provide the solution to a problem in a context of complete technocratic autonomy; nor to negotiate in secret with administrators, politicians, and possibly entrepreneurs to resolve the conflict between technology, management, and possibly real estate speculation while also looking toward creating more general and long-term well-being. Instead, their function would become that of stimulating and coordinating a process of popular participation through which the popular classes assume an authentic and crucial role in deciding the use and configuration of the territory. In this process, the urban planner evidently works in close relation with administrators and politicians, constituting an operational group in which tasks and competences are no longer juxtaposed but integrated, and in which, at any rate, delegation is replaced with direct and continuous accountability to the relevant community.

I would like to be clear on this point, so I shall add that the urban planner, in integrating their work with administrators and politicians, should not renounce their political position, in the same way that politicians and administrators should not renounce their prerogative to cast judgment on the urban planning process. Moreover, the urban planning, administrative, and political group that promotes and technically manages the operation should not be limited to passively accepting the requests that it receives from the participating community but should first open up channels for facilitating the community's full participation and then help it to work through its internal contradictions. The centuries-old deformation of the decision-making process has contaminated not only those who have the power to decide but also those who have been disempowered by it.

I insist again on this point because prudent reformers on the one hand and reckless demagogues on the other have in recent times been sowing a great deal of confusion. When urban planners enter into a participatory process, they will betray the participating community if they attempt to use paternalistic cunning to capture consensus, or if, taking a position of irresponsible acquiescence, they become acritical recorders of all requests they receive. The first instance is, as I have already said, mystifying; the second is doubly so. For not only does the latter evade the commitment to dialectically resolve the confrontation between competence (urban planner) and experience (community), but it completely removes the pole of competence from the confrontation (relieving the urban planner, who takes on the convenient function of an unproductive mediator, of the responsibility to have a deep knowledge of their field).

My point is that the urban planner, to successfully engage in a participatory process, must be infinitely more skilled and competent than those who operate traditionally under the umbrella of power: Their task is to stimulate awareness of an unjust state of affairs; to make collectively perceptible the motivations that lie behind such a state of affairs and the consequences it produces; to outline a new way of using and configuring the territory consistent with the real needs of the community; to propose organizational and morphological systems—in terms of physical, three-dimensional images—that express the values underpinning the real needs and expectations of the community; to contribute to defining a process of implementation and management of the mutually agreed interventions that is based on decentralization and the guidance of the social groups directly or indirectly involved. The complexity of this task requires planning skills and an aptitude for confrontation that can arise only from a rigorous educational experience that is scientific, political, and human. For it is only through such as process of experiential learning that one can acquire the ability to resolve the contradictions and ambiguities that inevitably emerge in the course of the urban planning process.

I will give an example, again taken from my experience in Rimini, of the difficulties posed by the problem of values. We conducted a preliminary survey on the significance that the city and its various parts had for its inhabitants, who were summarily grouped into different economic and social categories. One of the survey questions asked which building in Rimini the respondent considered most interesting. The answer was unanimous across all classes, all ages and both sexes: Leon Battista Alberti's Malatesta Temple. Certainly, the Malatesta Temple is an exceptional piece of architecture, stunning in the density of subtle meanings that it reveals through careful inspection; however, it is not "inhabited." The people of Rimini do not use it. I do not mean here from a functional point of view but in contemplative terms. The spaces around it are always deserted, and the promenade that leads to Piazza Tre Martiri runs along the opposite pavement, as if to avoid it.

Given this interesting finding, we furthered our analysis by drawing on a well-known procedure that attempts to approach the issue indirectly, such as by asking respondents to describe a given route which included the temple but without drawing their attention to it. This time the descriptions ignored the building that had previously been given as the most significant in the urban scene of Rimini. Other more modest buildings were listed, environments apparently devoid of value from the perspective of architecture or urban planning;

but no mention was made to Leon Battista Alberti's great work of architecture.

At this point, curiosity prompted us to take a look at the chronicles of the oldest newspaper collections—which we were already examining for other reasons—and with surprise we discovered that, from the mid-nineteenth century to the Red Week, every time a riot broke out in Rimini, the people ran to the Malatesta Temple and tore off its gratings, removed the stones from its base and smashed its window panes. Following a perhaps simplistic, but equally suggestive, line of thought, we can venture an interpretation to this singular instance of refusal to appropriate the temple. The Malatesta Temple had landed in Rimini like an unexpected space capsule. After securing his control over the city-state, Sigismondo Malatesta, riding on a wave of popular consensus, began to consolidate his power by following the typical procedure of appropriating and recycling the structures of the previous power. As often happens, the symbolic visualization of this operation was entrusted to a building, the author of which was Leon Battista Alberti.

Have you ever thought about the significance of that masterful envelope that imprisons the preexisting Gothic church while letting its presence transpire between the solids and voids of the two sides? It may be that, as far as Malatesta was concerned, the symbiosis between the two structures, made perfectly ambiguous by the reversal between content and container, already said enough. But for Alberti it was only a jumping-off point to develop the theme in stylistic terms through a paradoxical counterpoint of languages.

The only connection of the temple to its context passes through the Bridge of Tiberius and the Arch of Augustus, and this is an abstract reference since at the time the bridge was only an old bridge, and the arch was only a fornix in the walls used as a gate. But precisely because it lacks immediate concreteness, this connection becomes the origin of a complex circumvolution that leads to a state of total alienation, where formal expression achieves absolute purity and becomes a reflection of itself.

Looking at the temple, we ought to recognize that Malatesta's political expectations coincided precisely with Alberti's expressive research: The architecture materializes the rationale of power without any discontinuity, from the most directly content-oriented level to the subtlest level of linguistic associations. We ought also to recognize how in this work, Alberti, with more implacable determination than in other cases, went to great lengths to surround each of its components with alienness, down to the materials, technologies, and even the artisans, stonecutters, and masons: all imported and therefore foreign to the building traditions of the area.

So, perhaps, the refusal of appropriation by the popular classes in Rimini, which persists today, has remote and deep-rooted motivations.

I realize how paradoxical my interpretation may seem. And I know that if any academics were present at this conference, they would be horrified by the materialist crudity of my reasoning and its lack of idealistic grace. I would reassure them (as well as all of you) by saying that in my plan for the new city center I did not recommend the destruction of Alberti's temple. I consider it the most significant piece of architecture in the city and one of the most important pieces of cultural heritage in the world. Therefore, I proposed to reconstitute the urban fabric around it to place it in a more direct circuit of communicability.

The purpose of my remarks was not to discuss the Malatesta Temple but instead to draw your attention to a point that seems to me of fundamental importance. When an urban planning intervention is set up that seeks the participation of the popular classes, one's own values must be put on the table so that they can be debated by all the interlocutors. The interlocutors have their own, equally legitimate, values which must also be first brought to the surface and then jointly analyzed, with the same rigor with which one's own values are analyzed.

The Malatesta Temple is a borderline case for which it is clear from the outset that one could fight to the end to assert its inalienability, but there are many other cases for which value judgments are preconstituted and based on group or class prejudices or interests. In these cases, for participation to be real, one must be open to radical and profound revision.

On the other hand, there are also situations in which the interlocutors uphold values that are not their own but derive from images that are inculcated by the party opposed to them to serve their own ends. In these situations, too, a critical process of unveiling must penetrate to the core. As I have already said, participation means neither the capturing of consensus—that is, coercing others to accept one's judgments—nor neutral condescension—which serves to conceal technical incompetence and political disengagement. The aim of participation in urban planning is to bring social groups that have always been excluded into the decision-making processes that concern the transformation of the territory, and this aim can only be achieved if it is anchored in the foundation of a new value system corresponding to the ideological and pragmatic novelty that participation itself implies.

So, what has been done in this regard as part of the plan for the new center of Rimini? Many of you are familiar with the story, so I will briefly retrace it here.

We began with a series of meetings open to all citizens in the municipal *arengo*.[2] The themes addressed were based on a critical analysis of the various components that make up the territorial system of Rimini: from the structures characterizing the four belts (marina-center-periphery-countryside) to the subsystem of movement and transport and the subsystems of educational, health, commercial facilities, and so on. Each subsystem was critically analyzed in relation to all the others, highlighting how it had assumed its current configuration over time and what private or public decisions had determined it. For each subject of analysis, the approach was always the same: What use was made of the various spatial subsystems by the various groups of users; which groups of users had experienced and continued to experience benefits from the successive transformations of each subsystem and the overall system, and which ones instead experienced exclusion and exploitation? As the meetings went on, the picture that emerged was one of instrumental use of the land by a narrow social group that partially renewed itself over time without ceasing to be a minority and while maintaining their exclusive right to make decisions. Visible in the background of this picture was the connivance of technicians, always ingeniously subservient to the motives of power, and the awareness (in the worst cases) or unawareness (in the best cases) of administrators and politicians.

The meetings were a huge success. The conference halls of the city council, so often deserted (not only in Rimini, to be sure) by citizens inured to the contrived convolutions of international politics, were brimming with workers, intellectuals, clerks, professionals, students, and even peasants, passionately interested in participating in a new discussion on the real meaning of their city and territory.

However, in the discussions that followed the introductory presentations by Mayor Ceccaroni (who was enthusiastic about the new experience) and myself, the interventions mainly came from the intellectuals, who were usually more relaxed and often comfortable with the crowd, the microphones, and the speakers seated at the raised table. The others listened with great interest but did not intervene. The venue of the *arengo*, now democratic but once the seat of power, probably gave off an intimidating effect and discouraged those who lacked trust due to constantly been hustled to expose themselves too much—you never know.

Therefore, the decision was made to change the location of the meeting, a change that was, in any case, required also by the fact that the discussion was now becoming more and more specific.

So, we moved the discussion to various *case del popolo* in the city, the periphery, and the countryside—at the time the district councils did not exist yet.[3] The experience gained from these meetings was decisive for the formulation of the objectives of the plan and their transformation into proposals for the organization of the physical space. At the Che Guevara, in San Giuliano, in Covignano, and in the various districts of Marina, and so on, the problem of the future of the city and the role that the new center should play took on a concreteness that I had never experienced before. Urban planning became what it should always be: that is, a particular and specific aspect of a more general political discourse from which it cannot detach itself without becoming regressive and academic, or without losing the power of imagination that is indispensable to it.

The new trend that had begun to unfold did not fail to worry the hirelings and bureaucrats who did everything they could to close the channels through which the participation process was meant to spread.

Then came the local elections, the difficulties in forming the new city council, the shifts of balance in public institutions: Everything slowed down and, when it came to starting up again, the difficulties turned out to have been unexpectedly multiplied. Thus, drawing this discussion to a close, it can be said that, despite the tense and promising start, from a certain point onward not enough was done to open the road to participation in Rimini. If more had been done, namely what had been agreed, the struggle that broke out after the plan was adopted would have had a different outcome.

The Matteotti Village in Terni

Instead of dealing with the theme assigned to me in the abstract, I have chosen to relate it to a concrete case from my own personal experience. By doing so, I believe that the various underlying issues that relate to this theme may become clearer, even if the insights provided by the specific circumstances of the case I will refer to can only partially be generalized.

The case in question is a housing complex that I designed for the workers of The Steelworks in Terni at the beginning of the 1970s, of which so far only a first phase has been realized, corresponding to approximately a quarter of its overall extension.

1. The Premises of the Intervention

Terni is a city of 110,000 inhabitants in Umbria, located about 100 km northeast of Rome. The economic life of the city is centered on The Steelworks, which employs a workforce of more than seven thousand. The

Steelworks owned the area on which the intervention was to take place; it was not a vacant area, as is usually the case, but one already occupied by a residential neighborhood called Matteotti Village. In the year of its foundation, it had actually been christened Italo Balbo Village; that was in 1934, the fiftieth anniversary of The Steelworks and the twelfth of the Fascist era.[1] However, at the end of the Second World War, the company's management felt the need to change the toponymy and, to mark the advent of a new era, they hastened to complete the neighborhood—which was left unfinished since 1939—exactly as originally planned but with technically inferior buildings due to the postwar shortage of materials. When the project was drafted, the development of the southeastern quadrant of the city of Terni had not yet crossed the river Nera, so that the approximately twenty hectares of area allocated for the village was in open countryside. This provided the opportunity to build a "worker's ghetto" that was completely isolated from the urban context and that, if needed, was easily controllable.

Rumor has it that even Mussolini was involved in the case, that he examined the project and, after careful consideration, approved it, writing on one of the boards a recommendation that access to the road network servicing the houses be reduced to a minimum. Unfortunately, there is no evidence of this, which is a pity. For it could tell us something not only about the history of the political customs of the day but also serve to chronicle some subsequent approaches which—out of self-interest, demagogic inclination, or political laziness—had been disposed to reevaluating the village and preserving it as it was. Back then the planners had faithfully adhered to the objectives of their patrons; but, as is typical in such cases, they had tried to mediate the crudeness of the objectives with whatever cultural novelties they possessed. They managed to introduce just as many consolatory touches as needed to not only confuse the substance of the operation but also to serve as justification for a planning misdeed. While the responsibility for this misdeed was perhaps not entirely shared, it had nonetheless been tacitly accepted. The "concentrationary" structure of the village was sugarcoated by inserting echoes of models that many decades earlier had circulated in Western Europe before finally arriving in the Italian provinces, on the wave of socialist expansion in the years around the First World War. The models I am referring to are those of the "garden cities," misunderstood as peripheral archipelagos where the subaltern classes could be compensated for their uprooting from the countryside or their expulsion from urban centers with a bit of land to grow vegetables on.

The houses were placed along the service roads just far enough to make room for four small allotments, corresponding to the four accommodations contained in each two-storied house. The entrance to the two ground-floor flats, like those to the two first-floor flats, departed from each allotment, so that each family, while living in the same block, would be under the illusion of retaining that same privacy that one might have in a farmhouse in the countryside or in an urban village. Further, even the architectural language, in a style reminiscent of northern mining villages, took on regional accents from Umbria, to mitigate the harshness of the volumetric grid with the more familiar features of a cottage or stable. Today, walking around that part of the village that has not been touched by the new intervention, especially in the seasons when the roads are not covered with mud and the vegetation is lush, one might have the impression that, in spite of everything, the environment is welcoming. The work that inhabitants have done over more than forty years to open new windows, replace doors, paint walls, repair plasters, erect pergolas, grow flowers and plants, and so on, can give the impression of a certain variety, surely more stimulating than the gloomy order of many newer blocks looming on the horizon. This, however, is not enough to change the architectural and urban planning substance of the village, which, despite the patient effort of appropriation by the inhabitants, remains what it is: a squalid agglomeration of houses, all the same and all equally unhealthy, made up of flats with small rooms and no passageways, without toilets, dripping with damp on the ground floor, threatened by the presence of two canals that when flooded submerge the entire area and when dry litter it with rubbish and rats, fitted with rickety, tiny windows, poorly insulated from external temperature fluctuations, lacking regular foundations and therefore cracked, served by unpaved roads which are swampy in the winter and dusty in the summer, and lacking communal facilities apart from the bar kiosk and church located near the main entrance to the complex. The architectural and urban decay is matched, as usual, by progressive social deterioration. Those who did not have the necessary means to carry out repairs and alterations, went elsewhere: to the most depressed buildings in the city center or to those built by property speculators in the periphery, or to those subsidized first by INA-Casa and then by Gescal,[2] where they are worse off but at least are spared the anguish caused by a lack of maintenance. Thus, in the village—apart from a few exceptions—only the more affluent have stayed (who are generally no longer factory workers and, therefore, have the means to make improvements), as well as pensioners who cannot improve, or even change, their accommodation because the rent that they pay—or which, in any case, that they can pay—is lower than any state-subsidized social housing. The two distinct groups—the well-to-do and the very poor—behave differently and rarely communicate with each other, partly because the village offers no opportunity for socialization and exchange, but above all because their interests are at odds. Except, that is, for one point on which they apparently came to an agreement a few years ago: that of asking the Terni Society to sell them the property as a leasehold to be redeemed on the basis of the rent they paid. But even on this point, the motivations of the two groups differed: The better-off were moved by the fantasy of being able to own property in an area that had now become valuable, while the pensioners were moved by the fear of being left homeless following a transformation of the village. In fact, neither the fantasy of the former nor the fear of the latter was unfounded, for the expansion of the city had already reached the village, which now found itself an effective, or potential, part of its urban fabric.

In any case, the municipal master plan—drawn up by architect Mario Ridolfi in 1960—took note of all the internal and external conditions of the Matteotti Village and laid the foundations for its radical restructuring. The plan envisaged increasing the building density of the village area from the approximately 1.5 m^3/sqm of its current state to 3 m^3/sqm, while the surrounding areas were earmarked for a large belt around a new neighborhood of the same density, with which the village was to be integrated after undergoing redevelopment. It was precisely the provisions of the master plan that simultaneously fueled the fantasy of the wealthiest group and made the fear of the poorest seem plausible. The radical increase in the amount of buildable volume on each lot—along with the considerable location advantages that had objectively resulted from the expansion of the city center—greatly increased the potential value of the areas, making it negligible that the buildings on them were degraded and depreciated. Thus, if the flats were sold as leaseholds, it would have been impossible to avoid the risk of housing speculation taking over, acquiring lots, demolishing buildings, and then rebuilding them—using the new density permitted under the master plan—to sell them to tenants markedly different from those currently living in the village. Nor can it be assumed that the current tenants, once they acquired the advantages they had aspired to, would have resisted the speculative pressures; a few tempting offers concentrated on a few lots, possibly adjoining the 167-district envisaged by the municipality or the nearby private areas, where construction had already taken place according to the same master plan, would have likely been enough to breach any resistance. A carefully calculated distribution of speculative interventions—even in just a few spots—would have immediately broken up the village, making it more anachronistic than it already was.

2. Choosing the Type of Intervention

Faced with such a risky and contentious situation, in 1969—at the height of a period of awakening in Italian society—The Steelworks management and the factory councils became convinced of the need to immediately tackle the problem of the Matteotti Village. On the one hand, the management was willing to sell the houses to their tenants to shed once and for all the burden of having to intervene with heavy maintenance or, worse, renovation costs. On the other hand, the factory councils supported the idea of razing the complex to the ground and rebuilding on the same land the volume of housing permitted by the master plan. After lengthy discussions, with no resolution in sight between the two irreconcilable alternatives, the management decided to hand the problem over to an architect; that is, someone who could resolve it in purely technical, and therefore unequivocal, terms. But the architect—namely, myself—realized right away that if I were to cut the knot, instead of trying to untangle it, I would have found myself playing the ambiguous role of servant to a power I did not like. Therefore, I asked for the assignment to be postponed until all aspects of the issue had been further clarified and, in order to facilitate such a clarification, I proposed to study at my own risk the problem in order to draw from it more precise indications, on the basis of which not only the management, but also the factory councils, would be able to make an informed decision.

After a short time, five different proposals for intervention were presented: The first entailed a complete redevelopment of the village, providing it with the necessary collective facilities and radically renovating the residential buildings, yet without changing its original configuration; the second entailed replacing the original building structure with a system of tower blocks similar to a previous intervention that The Steelworks had carried out in a different area; the third also entailed a replacement, but this time with a building complex similar to those that social housing authorities built everywhere in Italy; the fourth and fifth proposed a more complex system consisting of three superposed decks into which a series of linear structures are excavated, including living quarters, services directly pertaining to housing, and channels for pedestrian movement. Each of the five alternatives came with a description of the benefits and drawbacks it implied, in relation to the different points of view that could be considered. The first alternative almost retained the original housing density (1.8 m^3/sqm), the second and the third were based on the density permitted by the master plan (3 m^3/sqm), while the fourth and fifth alternatives stayed below this density which was considered excessive (2.4 m^3/sqm). The five alternatives were handed in with a note stating that I would be interested in developing the project, and thus taking on the commission, only if the fourth or fifth solution was chosen: The first three could be implemented by The Steelworks on their own or by approaching others who shared their views. At this point, the discussion began within the factory with the participation of the trade unions and the political parties; it did not really come up against insurmountable prejudices, not least because at that time—albeit only for a brief period—there were a couple of open-minded individuals at the top of The Steelworks management who were eager to repair past abuses. Thus, the conclusion was to proceed with the fourth and fifth proposal and to accept their conditions. Some of these were technical (segregation of different types of movement; low building height and, hence, relatively high urban density; the presence of services as an extension of the living quarters and hence their incorporation into the residential fabric; intensive integration of greenery in the built-up area; high level of collective facilities), others were economic (higher costs—around 15 percent borne entirely by The Steelworks—based on the fact that the resources provided by the state would not allow for acceptable urban levels to be reached), and others were procedural (preemption rights for current retired tenants without increased economic burden; user participation in the entire design process). This last condition—that of user participation—had perhaps not been fully understood. On the contrary, at first it was probably interpreted as one of my many ploys to coopt the various beneficiaries of the project by letting them decide on minor details and to gloss over the substantive decisions made by funders and administrators. However, everyone soon realized—with astonishment and discontent—that this was far from a ploy, and that participation in an architectural event has a contagious effect, which can spread even into the ineffable spheres of the management of economic and political power. The operation was carried out based on the conditions accompanying the fourth and fifth proposal, and it is probably sufficient to indicate a few of the aspects which emerged from it.

3. The Project and Its Realization

Initially, we did not know who the actual users would be, since the mechanisms of allocation of social housing are designed in such a way that accommodations are distributed only when they are finished. Thus, we were compelled to address all the potential users, that is, all the workers who needed housing—around 1,800. The meetings were kickstarted by showing a range of realized projects regarded as acceptable, selected from various countries and not necessarily low cost. This disruptive trigger was intended to immediately shift the attention of the potential users toward models other than those that are normally offered and that influence peoples' imagination, that is, to make conflicts explode from the outset. And in fact, a conflict promptly erupted, immediately calling into question the objectives of the operation and forcing everyone, especially those who led the operation—the designer, the sociologist, the technical collaborators—to lay their cards on the table and to speak openly about any aspect of the operation and not only their specific expertise. In the recurrent meetings, held with consecutive small groups (during working hours and with no managers present), the discussion remained stuck for a long time on the background of the problem, which was tackled with genuine anger in all its human, political, and economic aspects, exploring the ways in which it was imprinted on the workers' conditions. But once a certain amount of clarity on the situation had been achieved, it was possible to begin the process by, firstly, defining the overall real needs on the basis of which the first proposals for restructuring the neighborhood were formulated and, secondly, defining the specific real needs on the basis of which the discussion on the configuration of the housing spaces could also begin.

It is difficult to separate the two aspects now, because in the design process they developed simultaneously and in response to each other. For the sake of convenience, we might say that the housing complex is treated as a set of superposed decks into which the networks of pedestrian and vehicular movement and the building grounds are excavated. The channels for vehicular movement are reduced to the minimum necessary for conveyance to residencies and services, hence running only along one side of the building grounds. On the other side run the channels of pedestrian movement on the ground, which can also be found on the opposite side at a raised level. The ground and elevated pedestrian channels are joined along the vertical connections servicing the flats, with ramps and stairs treated as open sloping paths. An additional system of elevated walkways connects transversally to the main pedestrian network, intersecting with the services supplementing the houses and bypassing the main traffic artery that spans the entire neighborhood. The building grounds are the sites where different typologies of buildings are located. To accommodate their placement, a three-dimensional grid has been defined, indicating the position of the vertical connections and the maximum permissible envelope of the buildings.

In the first phase of implementation, namely, the one that has already been built, the definition of the housing spaces became part of the participation process. Based on an initial assessment of needs, fine-tuned together with all potential users, five different housing units were defined, each consisting of three different hubs located on the three different floors, for which a total of fifteen alternative solutions were developed. Later, a second assessment of needs was developed with the real users (who, due to our request, had been designated while the complex was still under construction), which led to the introduction of three more variants within each hub. As a result, forty-five alternative solutions were provided for the two hundred and fifty flats under construction. In the next phase—if it is ever built—the housing types might be chosen from a catalogue that includes the alternative solutions of the first phase, minus those that will have been eliminated and plus those that will have been suggested based on the experience of use, and with the further addition of those that will emerge from a new assessment of the needs of future users. And so on until the fourth phase—which was meant to be the last—in which my contribution as designer would not be to design the whole complex but to study its junctions and its necessary adjustments in relation to the spatial grid. The issue of designing the whole complex was not even raised in the first phase because the frequency and pace of the different housing units was determined by the users. In this sense, the superposed decks, the three-dimensional grid, and the modulation of the housing units imparted a sort of intellectual discipline on the complex, punctually contradicting any inclination toward automatisms or mechanical materializations. User participation was constant throughout the process and led to decisions on the structure and form of the event being designed. Yet, it grew discontinuous during the execution of the works (from which, in any case, even myself as the designer had been officially excluded) when it should have served as an instrument of rigorous control; all the more so since the contractor and construction management, who belonged to the same state-owned firm as the client (Finsider), were caught up in an ambiguous relationship of cronyism that by no means allowed for open disagreements, however objective these might be. It has picked up again, albeit less intensely, since the experience of using the building began. At this point, its intensification would have been of great importance to record feedback and carry the operation forward while continuing to correct it. Yet, the urge for radical renewal that characterized the late 1960s is now a distant memory. Many things have changed at The Steelworks: The managers who overcame their initial doubts and ended up sincerely supporting a new way of shaping the physical environment of their workers have been replaced. Unless the political and administrative situation changes, it is unlikely that the first phase of the new Matteotti Village will be followed by the other planned phases. In fact, as things stand, this can be ruled out altogether, which is a shame because the first phase is too small, lacks the general services that should have been implemented after the second phase, and remains an island floating in the sea of the old village, which is still as dilapidated and alien as it was at the start.

4. Lights and Shadows on the Role of Different Social Constituencies

To conclude and to highlight some significant aspects, which, for better or worse, have marked my experience, I shall add a few observations on the relationships that developed between the whole design process and the social constituencies—not only the public ones—which were directly or indirectly involved. Starting with the group of working-class families for whom the houses were built, I must say that their participation was fundamental and had a decisive impact on the project. While they did not really influence the project's linguistic elements—which are, of course, my own as the architect—they provided the substrate on which the organization of space was articulated. Had we not been in constant dialogue with these families, certain ideas dictated by real needs or cultural inclinations (terrace gardens, the independence of dwellings, the variety of organizational configurations, etc.) would not have emerged. In fact, without their struggle, it would have been impossible to get The Steelworks management to agree on spending a little more to improve the quality of the work, to reduce maintenance and operational costs, and to implement services as an extension of the living quarters. Unfortunately, this involvement waned as the operation drew to a close—especially when the users were excluded from overseeing the finances of the project's construction in the name of their alleged technical incompetence—and was dealt a final blow when it was decided that the flats would be sold off rather than rented out. A rather complex procedure had been devised to establish a rental method that would give guarantees to the tenants both in terms of legal rights of usership and in economic terms, while leaving the property and thus also the maintenance costs to the company. Both management and the factory councils had been convinced of the soundness of the procedure; but then, unexpectedly, the CISL raised the flag of ownership and the CGIL, fearing it had been outflanked, snatched it out of their hands and became its standard bearer.[3] Thus, any other proposal was shelved, and the users became owners before the houses were even finished. Since then, there has been talk of raising fences, of sectioning off footpaths to turn them into balconies, of possible upward extension rights. Even more seriously, a rift has opened between the group of workers who would immediately own the housing and the much larger group of those who would have to wait a long time: The bonds of solidarity that had made this operation so successful were thus abruptly severed. As for the factory councils, it is thanks to them that the whole operation of participation took place with such intensity. It is also thanks to them that disputes with the company's bureaucratic apparatus were resolved in favor of the future users of the housing complex. The same cannot be said of the trade unions, which, on the contrary, consumed by mutual rivalries, often policed and exercised a restraining influence on their members. The city's left-wing administration has had only one concern throughout the whole operation: not to compromise itself with an intervention that, had it succeeded, could have been seen as a change for the better in the management of The Steelworks. Clinging to the image of The Steelworks management as the incarnation of absolute evil, it has done everything in its power not to facilitate the operation. One can assume that this is still the case, given that even today it has not granted licenses to those few businesses included in the residential buildings, nor has it put into operation the three public services that were included in the first phase of implementation. Furthermore, perhaps due to an ill-judged electoral calculation, it was never keen to displease the group of wealthy tenants of the old neighborhood who demanded ownership of their houses, and it made a show of listening to their demands as the Curia and the Christian Democrats already did with conviction. The Steelworks management, at the time headed by a progressive chief executive officer and a progressive chief technical officer, deserves credit for embracing the idea of advanced urban planning. But in doing so, the two progressives set themselves on a path fraught with the shadiest kinds of sabotage. The group to which The Steelworks belongs was not in agreement, and neither was the internal bureaucratic structure; what they did agree on was that the two inconvenient characters had to be got rid of as soon as possible. Indeed, this dismissal punctually occurred following a savage takeover, which took place before the first phase of the project was completed. The only constituency left to discuss is Gescal, responsible for administering the assets made available by the ECSC (European Coal and Steel Community) for the construction of the first two hundred fifty houses. The European body had set one condition for the use of those funds: that some interesting experimentation be introduced in the project's construction. Gescal suggested that this be fulfilled by adopting a steel beam designed by its technicians capable of bearing loads over a span of 2.50 meters, as well as a full-height window panel of the type that has been used in the most respectable apartment blocks in Italy since 1945. Much effort went into persuading Gescal that the beam and window panel, as experiments, were insignificant. In the end, we succeeded. The obstacle was brilliantly circumvented by proclaiming that what was experimental in the Matteotti Village was the participation of users in the project.

Notes

Introduction

1. I am indebted here to the work of Stefan Collini. In his sustained engagement with the history of higher education, the British academic challenges the idea of a "true university," emphasizing instead its shifting forms and purposes over time: "No decade," he writes, "can plausibly be chosen to represent the 'normal' condition of the system." Yet he discerns a notable continuity between the foundational principles of universities in early nineteenth-century Europe and their substantial expansion in the three decades following 1945, a continuity defined by a shared commitment to open-ended inquiry and a persistent inclination to serve practical end. Stefan Collini, *What Are Universities For?* (Penguin, 2012), 22; and *Speaking of Universities* (Verso, 2017).

2. For a cursory, yet panoramic, analysis of the different types of relationship contemporary universities maintains with their respective nation-states across the world, see the first chapter of Stefan Collini, *What Are Universities For?* . Collini is dubious about the existence of a contemporary global university, yet he points to "the concomitant introduction of similar organizational and financial arrangements which cut across, and have sometimes signalled major departures from, existing national traditions." Collini, 14.

3. Literature on the neoliberal turn of British universities is vast, but for a first-hand account elaborated in the aftermath of the tripling of fees on the part of Labour's government in the early 2000, see Andy McGettigan, *The Great University Gamble: Money, Markets and the Future of Higher Education* (Pluto, 2013). For more recent analysis, consider the special issue of *Radical Philosophy*'s dossier "Unmaking the University," 2021; Peter Fleming, *Dark Academia: How Universities Die* (Pluto, 2021); the ongoing enquiry of Stefan Collini, culminated in the key books *What Are Universities For?* and his more recent *Speaking of Universities* (Verso, 2017). Among the latest journalistic reporting on UK universities, I want to signal Lorna Finlayson's interventions in the *London Review of Books*, and in particular her article, "Everyone Hates Marking," *London Review of Books* 45, no. 6, March (2023), and "Car Park Education" published on the

October 9, 2024, on the LRB blog, shttps://www.lrb.co.uk/blog/2024/october/car-park-education, accessed November 2024.

4. Another academic perspective on student protests in the 1960s and 1970s is found in E. P. Thompson's edited work, *Warwick University Ltd: Industry, Management and the Universities* (Penguin Education Special, 1970).

5. De Carlo in Filippo De Pieri, 'Il breve e il lungo '68 di Giancarlo De Carlo' in Giancarlo De Carlo, *La piramide rovesciata. Architettura oltre il '68* (Quodlibet, 2018), 21.

6. The talk was part of the "Venerdì letterari" (Literary Fridays), a program of public events that featured the participation of prominent cultural representatives of the time.

7. De Carlo in De Pieri, *La piramide rovesciata*, 16.

8. Tom Holert, *Politics of Learning, Politics of Space: Architecture and the Education Shock of the 1960s and 1970s* (De Gruyter, 2021).

9. Cedric Price, "ATOM. Design for New Learning for a New Town," *AD* (May 1968): 232. Price had already explored the idea of an architecture of parts in two earlier projects: the National School Plan (NSP) and the famous Potteries Thinkbelt, both dated 1966.

10. See Michael Pearson, "Enclosures for Learning," and John E. Tirrell and Albert A. Canfield, "Goodbye to the Classroom," both in *AD* (May 1968).

11. Unauthored, "New Tools. Education's Emerging Technology," "The School Scene: Change and More Change," special issue of *Progressive Architecture* (April 1968), 135.

12. Wilbur Schramm, "Communication Satellites for Learning," *AD* (May 1968), 212. The text is excerpted from the paper "Communication Satellites for Education, Science and Culture," Reports and Papers on Mass Communication 53 (Paris: UNESCO).

13. For the sake of intellectual honesty, it is important to mention that the editorial of the April issue of *PA* expressed some concerns about "education . . . [being] asked to purify all our national problems of racial injustice, violence, poverty, and hatred." However, such a concern remained underexplored, and the editorial line of the magazines implicitly abided by the prospect of educational architecture's becoming a tool of governmentality.

14. De Carlo, 'Architecture's Public', 89, in this volume.

15. For a detailed description of the unfolding of the events from 1963 onward, see the catalogue of the exhibition *La rivoluzione culturale: la Facoltà di architettura del Politecnico di Milano 1963–1974*, held at the Politecnico di Milano in 2009. The digital version of the catalogue, printed internally on that occasion was made available at http://www.gizmoweb.org/wp-content/uploads/2009/10/la-rivoluzione-culturale-catalogo-bassa-protetto.pdf. Accessed September 9, 2022. On the same topic, also consider Marco Biraghi, Gabriella Lo Ricco, Silvia Micheli, Mario Viganò (eds.), *Italia 60–70. Una stagione dell'architettura* (Il Poligrafo, 2009) and Lucia Tenconi, *The City and Its Social Problems as a Subject of Study: Rebel Architects at the Faculty of Milan (1963–1973)*, in Pieter Dhondt and Elizabethanne Boran (eds.), *Student Revolt, City, and Society in Europe. From the Middle Ages to the Present* (Routledge, 2017).

16. I refer, here, to a series of pictures of the 1963 occupation of the Milan Polytechnic by Walter Barbero held in the Barbero Archive in Bergamo. Archive visited in May 2024.

17. The self-management of the faculty, initiated in December 1967, led to an educational experiment based on the organization of research groups involving professors, assistants, and students working together on a common theme. In this context, De Carlo, alongside Paolo Ceccarelli, coordinated a research project titled *Notes on Urban Planning Legislation*, which provided a detailed analysis of the content of Italy's main urban planning laws. See De Pieri, 'Il breve e il lungo '68 di Giancarlo De Carlo' in Giancarlo De Carlo, *La piramide rovesciata. Architettura oltre il '68* (Quodlibet, 2018), 20.

18. Consider notes 9, 10, 11, and 12.

19. De Carlo, *The Overturned Pyramid*, 8, in this volume.

20. De Carlo, *The Overturned Pyramid*, 41, in this volume.

21. G. De Carlo and F. Bunčuga, *Conversazioni su architettura e libertà* (Elèuthera, 2018), 58.

22. For a detailed account of De Carlo's political activity during the Second World War and on his subsequent interest in anarchist theory and practice, see Giancarlo De Carlo and Franco Bunčuga, *Conversazioni su architettura e libertà* (2018).

23. Consider, in particular, from page 75 to 81 in Bunčuga, *Conversazioni su architettura e libertà* (2018).

24. Alongside *The Overturned Pyramid*, he published *Pianificazione e disegno delle università* (Edizioni Universitarie Italiane, 1968).

25. De Carlo cocurated with Alberto Rosselli and the MID group the section "Information." "Errors" was curated by Albe Steiner and Marco Zanuso and "Perspectives" by Vittoriano Viganò, Pino Tovaglia, and Livio Castiglioni. See Pica Agnoldomenico (ed), *Catalogo della XIV Triennale* (1968).

26. Silvia Paoli (ed), *Cesare Colombo, Photographs 1952–2012* (Silvana Editoriale, 2020), 146.

27. Unauthored photograph, held at the Milan Triennale Archive, consulted May 2024, available via the Lombardia Beni Culturali digital archive: https://www.lombardiabeniculturali.it/fotografie/schede/IMM-3u040-0003057/?view=ricerca&offset=298.

28. Paola Nicolin, *Castelli di carte: la XIV Triennale di Milano, 1968* (Quodlibet, 2011), 27. By the same author also consider: "'Beyond the Failure: Notes on the 24th Triennale," *Log* 13/14, Aftershocks: Generation(s) Since 1968 (Fall 2008): 87–100.

29. "Una 'scalata' contro la cultura del sistema, intervista a Giancarlo De Carlo," *L'Unità*, (June 12, 1968): 8.

30. Lucia Tenconi, "The City and Its Social Problems, as a Subject of Study: Rebel Architects at the Faculty of Milan (1963–1973)," Pieter Dhondt, Elizabethanne Boran (eds), *Student Revolt, City, and Society in Europe. From the Middle Ages to the Present* (Routledge, 2017).

31. Giancarlo De Carlo, "Why/How to Build School Buildings," *Harvard Educational Review* 39, no. 4 (1969): 12–35, now in *La piramide rovesciata* (Quodlibet, 2018).

32. De Carlo, "Why/How to Build School Buildings," 88, in this volume.

33. Richard Saul Wurman (ed.), "Making the City Observable," *Design Quarterly* 80 (1971).

34. Colin Ward, Anthony Fyson, *Streetwork: The Exploding School* (Routledge & K. Paul, 1973).

35. Ward's and Wurman's contribution to this strand of research exceeds the publications listed in the main text. We should mention that Ward was coeditor of the *Bulletin of Environmental Education* between 1971 and 1979, while in the same years Wurman was appointed director of the 1972 International Design Conference in Aspen, which he devoted to the city as a learning environment. The proceedings of the conference were published in issue 86 of *Design Quarterly*.

36. De Carlo, "Why/How to Build School Buildings," 58, in this volume.

37. I owe this excellent point to Adam Wood, "Giancarlo De Carlo: How to Keep Educational Architecture Human or Creative Anti-Institutionalism," June 28, 2018. https://architectureandeducation.org/2018/06/28/giancarlo-de-carlo-how-to-keep-educational-architecture-human-or-creative-anti-institutionalism/. Accessed on October 20, 2022.

38. See John Dewey, *Experience and Education* (Macmillan, 1938).

39. De Carlo, "Architecture's Public," 123, in this volume.

40. See in particular: Paul Davidoff, "Advocacy and Pluralism in Planning." *Journal of the American Institute of Planners* 31, no. 4 (1965): 331–338; Paul and Linda Davidoff, "Opening the Suburbs: Toward Inclusionary Land Use Controls," *Syracuse Law Review* 22 (1970): 509–536.

41. Giancarlo De Carlo's essay, "An Architecture of Participation," was published in 1972 by the Royal Australian Institute of Architects as part of the Melbourne Architectural Papers series. Giancarlo De Carlo's 'Progettazione e partecipazione. Il caso di Rimini' was originally published in De Carlo at al., *Le radici malate dell'urbanistica italiana* (Moizzi, 1976). 'Il Villaggio Matteotti a Terni' was initially published in Lodovico Meneghetti (ed.), *Introduzione alla cultura della città* (Clup, 1981). We refer here to the version of the essay published by Quodlibet in the 2015 *L'Architettura della partecipazione*, which is translated in this anthology.

42. De Carlo, 'The Architecture of Participation', 145, in this volume.

43. Domenico de Masi, "Partecipazione e progetto," in Maria Rita Guccione and Alessandra Vittorini (eds.), *Giancarlo De Carlo. Le ragioni dell'architettura* (2005), 66–67.

44. De Carlo, 'The architecture of participation', 156, in this volume.

45. It's important to remember that from 1978 to 2001, De Carlo directed the Italian edition of the French magazine *Espaces et sociétés*, cofounded by Henri Lefevbre and Anatole Kopp in 1970.

46. Lefebvre, *The Production of Space* (Basil Blackwell, 1991).

47. De Carlo, "Architecture's Public," 111, in this volume. Originally published in *Parametro* I, 5 (1970): 4–12.

48. De Carlo, "Architecture's Public," 112, in this volume.

49. De Carlo, "The Matteotti Village in Terni," 215, in this volume.

The Overturned Pyramid

1. This paper was developed in the framework of a conference held by the Italian Cultural Association (Associazione Culturale Italiana) in several cities during the first week of February 1968. In the short span of a month, the revolt has spread to other faculties, reaching new layers of students, with its goals getting broader and more precise by the day. The present analysis does not claim to have recorded everything nor provides any definitive conclusions. The movement, fortunately, is so rapid and intense as to render that task impossible.

2. In his 1810 note *On the Internal and External Organisation of the Higher Scientific Institutions in Berlin*, Wilhelm von Humboldt argues that "institutes of higher education must regard science as a permanently unresolved problem . . . as a field of knowledge that is not yet and never can be discovered, although it needs to be investigated as if it could be fully discovered."

3. Napoleon I added: "In well-organized states, there is always a body destined to address the principles of morality and politics: this function has been performed by the University of Paris and the Sorbonne in France, Pavia, Pisa, and Padua in Italy, Göttingen and Jena in Germany, Salamanca in Spain, Oxford in England, the Ulama in Turkey; these bodies have always been the ultimate defenders of the moral cause and the principles of the State."

4. The Gentile Reform, in its first draft, contained very precise references to the idealistic framework outlined by Fichte in his *A Plan, Deducted from First Principles, for an Institution of Higher Learning to Be Established in Berlin*, according to which the university, as an institutionalized place for the transmission of truth, was to be guaranteed the strictest isolation from the contingencies of the surrounding world.

5. Trans. note: De Carlo is referring here to Bill no. 2314, better known as the "Gui Reform." Presented in May 1965 by the then Minister of Education Luigi Gui, the proposed reform of the university system was deemed inadequate to solve the problems posed by the transformation of the university into a mass institution open to all high school graduates. The bill was promptly met with the opposition of the student assemblies and became one of the themes around which the student protest would gather.

6. The students have never bothered, in the course of their struggle, to attack the internal configuration of the academic structure (except for the immediate repercussions it might have had on them), as if changing it were none of their business, or rather as if its destruction could only be an implicit consequence of dismantling the more general structure of the university. This position is interesting and reveals political maturity and breadth. But it is also interesting that no group of lecturers, even those who are closest to the positions of the students, has ever agreed to question the mechanisms that govern academic privilege. At every faculty meeting, when looking for ways to support the student movement, all good intentions always evaporated when someone came out and said that perhaps the best way to help students was to attack the professorial power structure from within.

7. In climbing the academic pyramid, the secret for a rapid success is being able to endure hiding one's thoughts for years. The fact is that—in most cases—the burden of endurance gets progressively lighter and lighter, until eventually the achievement of success coincides with having nothing left to think about.

8. Trans. note: Morotean refers to the political faction of the Christian Democrats—the then ruling party—that was close to Prime Minister Aldo Moro and represented more left-leaning positions.

9. Introduced in France in 1966, the Fouchet plan has reformed the education of the humanities and sciences. Its stated purpose is to favor the most deserving and support greater specialization; its true purpose is to bring about a classist culture and provide instrumental executives to industry and administration according to their various requirements. The education system is divided into three cycles: The first is the same for all; the second trains specialists destined for generic research and teaching; the third corresponds to the doctorate level.

The most important filter lies between the first and second cycle: The less talented stop there and are encouraged to move on to higher technical institutes, which can also be accessed directly from middle school. The second cycle is divided into two sections: the short cycle, from which a diploma is obtained that allows the individual to teach in secondary schools, and the long cycle, which leads to a master's degree that permits university teaching and research.

One of the objectives of the struggle raging in French universities today is the replacement or revision of this mechanism, considered technocratic, segregationist, and classist.

10. The parting of the student movement from the established political forces, including those of the extreme left, has worsened, especially during the last few episodes. The communist press, which was very prompt in declaring itself in agreement with each step forward, could not hide its puzzlement and disappointment toward the report that Turin students Bobbio and Viale presented at the National Convention of Representatives of the Occupied University on March 10 and 11 in Milan. Yet this position, much more widely shared than the press has noted, is undoubtedly the richest in revolutionary content.

11. Some statements recorded recently by a journalist from the newspaper *Europeo* clarify even better the new political and cultural perspectives opened up by the students: "What we need to achieve is not so much a charter of demands and their implementation but the definite overhaul of the professor as an authority figure in the University, so that we [students] are enabled to participate as equals in the formative process of our culture. . . . What we call student power consists not in the fact that we already know how to run the University, but in the fact that we can already debate it. . . . It is perfectly true that two and two makes four, but four what? That's what we want to know."

12. In fact, the first occupation of a Faculty of Architecture took place in Venice in 1958, when the state certification exam was introduced.

13. Many Faculties of Architecture experienced before others the phenomenon, that was later generalized, of Faculty Boards, in the moment of danger, accepting to expand the board to include adjunct professors and even assistants with the dual purpose of engaging them in mediation and diluting their responsibilities. Once the danger had passed, either by agreement or through police intervention, the intruders were immediately expelled.

14. The typical attitude of Black Power is that students reject any kind of help offered by professors, even the least suspicious. Stokely Carmichael said: "Many [whites] have come seeing no difference in color, they have come 'color blind.' But at this time and in this land [the USA] color *is* a factor and we should not overlook or deny this. The black organizations do not need this kind of idealism, which borders on paternalism." (Trans. note: Stokely Carmichael and Charles V. Hamilton, "Chapter 3: The Myths of Coalition" in *Black Power: The Politics of Liberation* (Random House, 1967).

15. It is symptomatic that the Faculties of Architecture were absent from the urban planning debate of the 1960s in which the territorial future of the country was being played out. While the battle over intermunicipal plans and a new urban planning law raged on, only feeble complaints emerged from faculty members about the formal disregard of the results achieved.

16. Trans. note: Charenton was a lunatic asylum founded in 1645 by the Frères de la Charité (Brothers of Charity) in Charenton-Saint-Maurice, now Saint-Maurice, Val-de-Marne, France. Charenton is most famously known as the final resting place of the Marquis de Sade. Peter Weiss's 1963 play *The Persecution and Assassination of Jean-Paul Marat as Performed by the Inmates of the Asylum of Charenton Under the Direction of the Marquis de Sade* (usually shortened as *Marat/Sade*) dramatizes the fact that de Sade, an inmate at the facility, used to direct plays featuring other inmates as actors.

17. The concept of the department, whose definition was already confused in the Gui bill, has reached its highest levels of mystification in the Faculty of Architecture. Expanding on Gui's idea of the department as a larger institute, some arrived at the dream of the department of *Panarchitecture*: where courses in urban planning, design, science and technology would be supplemented by courses in sociology, economics, geography, and so on, so as to create a host of auxiliaries, all serving a few star architects engaged in architectural composition.

18. The open curriculum implies self-management of the university by students. This prospect—which most professors find abominable, since it would represent the destruction of their extra-cultural powers—is in fact not so remote in many foreign universities where students already manage all the school's services and intervene decisively in the definition of programs and the choice of professors.

At this current stage of the debate, the demand for self-management proposed by the most advanced part of the student movement seems to be the main obstacle to reaching an agreement. The counterproposal of the Faculty Boards puts forward forms of equal comanagement that rely on the favorable alliances that would occur in mixed assemblies where three-quarters of the participants are still subject to the influence of academic dealings.

Self-management and comanagement are the two poles of a conflict that crosses the boundaries between party and counterparty, seeping into the students' camp and dividing it into two opposite tendencies.

19. In those Faculties of Architecture where the Faculty Boards have formally agreed to turn every activity into research, none of these three prerequisites was taken into consideration. On the contrary, attempts were made to set up very large groups with the pretext of giving the greatest number of students the opportunity to participate; the most heterogenous and obvious topics were chosen with the pretext of trying to immerse these groups in the surrounding reality to fully grasp it; and the groups were structured along the traditional military methods that have always been employed in Italian universities.

20. As Pier Paolo Pasolini observes in "Laboratorio" (*Nuovi Argomenti*, January–March, 1966): "Internal revolutions would work physically in the masses—through a kind of anthropological transformation—starting from oral languages downwards; external revolutions, on the other hand, would operate mainly and primarily in the special languages of the elites"; "The 'langue' . . . does not only evolve regularly (as the socio-political establishment implies) but can also undergo revolutionary change. This happens when the establishment breaks down and enters a crisis of development due to a revolution that it created."

21. The broadening of architecture's field of action has led to the proposal of encouraging the segmentation of the current faculty into three new distinct faculties: Industrial Design, Architecture, and Urban Planning. Besides repeating the shortcomings of the existing situation three times over, this operation would have the effect of destroying the common matrix of the three activities without succeeding in defining their respective conceptual and instrumental autonomy. In this sense, it should be considered as a mirror image of the operation of pan-architecture. Both move from the assumption that the architectural material is either one or three and differ only in the weight they attribute to the unity or trinity of their alternate appearance. In reality, architectural activity has a broader scope and is further permeable to the penetration of other activities that converge around its own field of interests; therefore, only a broad and flexible pedagogical articulation within a unified context of studies can solve the problem.

Why/How to Construct School Buildings

1. A few years ago, in a Faculty of Architecture in the United States, some students worked on a remarkable school organization project aimed for urban contexts. Its basic idea was to organize special teaching equipment on self-propelled vehicles that could move around the city and in turn reach the schools when needed. Once again, the organization was divided into two parts: the set of fixed school buildings in various areas of the city and the fleet of mobile special equipment that could be combined with the former in constantly variable arrangements. Notably, this treatment of special equipment allows them to be used at their full capacity and thus makes it possible to refine them according to the highest technological level with no waste.

2. The centuries-old history of marginalizing people from the process of transforming the physical environment has created the ingrained opinion that there is little room for direct intervention and collective expression. The models developed by the ruling classes now appear to have no alternatives, such that the functional, organizational, and aesthetic principles they are based on appear as the only possibilities. This clouding of consciousness and perception engenders feelings of alienation, so that even in the rare cases in which direct action is possible, people continue to choose typologies and languages of expression that are entirely similar to those already set.

3. For concrete examples, one can look at how students in the architecture departments at Yale or MIT transformed their workplaces when they were able to take possession of them ("The Architectural Form," July–August 1967, and "Architectural Design," August 1968); but even more significant is what can be discovered about the student revolts in universities and secondary schools by leafing through French, German, and Italian magazines from 1968.

Architecture's Public

1. Trans. note: CIAM is the acronym of Congrès Internationaux d'Architecture Moderne, or the International Congress of Modern Architecture. Founded in 1928 and disbanded in 1959, the organization was responsible for a series of events and congresses convened across Europe by the most prominent architects of the time, with the objective of spreading the principles of the modern movement focusing on the main domains of architecture (such as housing, landscape, urbanism, industrial design, etc.).

The Architecture of Participation

1. Trans. note: De Carlo is referring to Robert Venturi and Denise Scott Brown who, at the time of writing, had just published "A Significance for A&P Parking Lots, or Learning from Las Vegas," *Architectural Forum* (March 1968): 37–43. This article later became the first chapter of *Learning from Las Vegas*

(Cambridge, MA: MIT Press, 1972). The book, coauthored with Steven Izenour, has become a pop culture classic.

Planning and Participation: The Case of Rimini

1. Trans. note: The Red Week was a week of popular unrest which occurred June 7–14, 1914. Over seven days, widespread rioting and largescale strikes erupted throughout the Italian provinces of Romagna (where Rimini is located) and Marche. The rioters were protesting a series of antiworker reforms introduced in 1914 by the previous prime minister, Giovanni Giolitti.

2. Trans. note: *Arengo* refers both to the assembly of citizens of a city-state in medieval Italy and to the place where they assembled.

3. Trans. note: *Case del popolo* (which literally translates to "houses of the people") are community centers that played an important role in popular Italian life as places for socialization, education, popular culture, and neighborhood activism. From the end of the nineteenth century, *case del popolo* emerged as places of congregation, owned and managed collectively by ordinary citizens, mostly located in the central regions of Emilia-Romagna and Tuscany.

The Matteotti Village in Terni

1. Trans. note: Giacomo Matteotti (1885–1924) was an Italian socialist politician who, after denouncing the frauds committed by the fascists in the 1924 general election, was kidnapped and killed by the secret police of Benito Mussolini. Italo Balbo (1896–1940) was an Italian fascist politician and leader of the Blackshirts, who served as Italy's marshal of the air force, governor-general of Italian Libya, and commander-in-chief of Italian North Africa.

2. Trans. note: INA-Casa refers to the Italian state's intervention plan to build public housing throughout Italy, conceived in the immediate postwar period and in force between 1949 and 1963. It was then replaced by Gescal (an acronym for *Gestione case per i lavoratori,* or Workers' Housing Management), a fund destined for the construction and allocation of houses to workers.

3. Trans. note: CISL (Italian Confederation of Trades Unions) and CGIL (Italian General Confederation of Labor) are two of the major national trade union confederations in Italy. CGIL was formed in 1944, by an agreement among socialists, communists, and Christian democrats. In 1950, socialists and Christian democrats split, forming UIL and CISL, respectively. As such, CISL represented various Catholic-inspired groups linked with the Christian Democracy Party (DC), while CGIL was mostly influenced by the Italian Communist Party (PCI).

Sources

The Overturned Pyramid

The book was published as the eighth volume in the series Dissensi (Dissents), De Donato, Bari 1968. It bears the inscription "Printed on 18 April 1968."

A typewritten version of the text ("Text submitted to De Donato"), dated March 16, 1968, is held at IUAV-AP (University of Venice IUAV—Project Archive), De Carlo-scritti/088.

In addition to the text reproduced here (5–73), the volume included a Biographical Note (74) and an appendix (75–199) of documents relating to the protests in the Italian Faculties of Architecture, preceded by the following warning: "The documents reproduced hereinafter, with the exception of some of particular historical interest, belong to the last period of struggle in our Faculties of Architecture (February–March 1968). As such, they do not claim to offer a complete documentation."

The index of documents reproduced in the appendix of the De Donato edition is as follows:

Milan

Public statement of the students of the Faculty of Architecture (February 15, 1963); motion unanimously approved by the Assembly of Architecture students (January 26, 1967); Faculty of Architecture of the Polytechnic University of Milan. Document of the assembly of the signatories (February 16, 1968); motion approved by the student assembly of the Faculty of Architecture, Milan (March 4, 1968); Motion presented (but not approved) to the assembly of the signatories of the Faculty of Architecture, Milan (March 14, 1968).

Venice

The occupied Faculty of Architecture. Public statement no. 1 (March 1, 1968); Public statement no. 2 (March 3, 1968); Public statement no. 3 (March 6, 1968); Motion passed by the general assembly of the students at Venice University Institute of Architecture, IUAV (March 14, 1968).

Turin

Conclusion of the talks between assistants and students at the June 1967 sessions (June 22–28, 1967); motions approved by the General Assembly of the students of the Faculty of Architecture: 1 (June 16, 1967), 2 (January 17, 1968), 3 (February 27, 1968), 4 (March 8, 1968).

Naples

Notes issued by the UGI (Italian Goliardic Unit) Architecture (February 9, 1968); the Left Manifesto for Architecture (February 27, 1968); motion passed by the Student Assembly of the Faculty of Architecture (March 8, 1968).

Rome

The Faculty of Architecture occupied. Motions: 1 (February 3, 1968), 2 (February 9, 1968); notes presented to the student assembly of the Faculty of Architecture (February 1968); document by the Commission "A" of the student assembly of the Faculty of Architecture (February 1968); working outline presented to the student assembly of the Faculty of Architecture (February 12, 1968).

Florence

Assembly of the Faculty of Architecture (January 30, 1968); motions approved by the student assembly of the Faculty of Architecture: 1 (February 12, 1968), 2 (February 26, 1968), 3 (March 4, 1968).

Palermo

Working proposals approved by the student assembly of the Faculty of Architecture (March 8, 1968); motion approved by a majority vote of the assembly of students, professors and assistants of the Faculty of Architecture (March 15, 1968); motion approved by the student assembly of the Faculty of Architecture (March 16, 1968).

Why/How to Construct School Buildings

The text was written in Italian but first published in Lynne Wilson's English translation as "How/Why to Build School Buildings" in *Harvard Educational Review* 39, no. 4 (1969): 12–34.

A typescript of the Italian text, bearing the title *Perché/come costruire edifici scolastici*, is held at IUAV-AP, De Carlo-scritti/096. A typescript of the English translation is also held at IUAV-AP, De Carlo-scritti/097.

The Italian version of the article was published on two occasions under different titles: "Ordine-istituzione educazione-disordine" (Order-institution education-disorder), *Casabella* 368–369 (1972): 65–71; *Perché/come costruire edifici scolastici*, in Giancarlo De Carlo, *Gli spiriti dell'architettura* (Architecture's Spirits), edited by Livio Sichirollo (Rome: Editori Riuniti, 1992), 201–221.

The version reproduced here restored (based on the typescript) footnote 3 of the original text, which was included in the English edition but omitted from the 1972 and 1992 Italian reprints.

Architecture's Public

The article was published in a bilingual Italian/English version, but without a title for the English version, in *Parametro* I, 5 (1970): 4–12.

A typescript of the Italian version is held at IUAV-AP, De Carloscritti/094. A typescript of the English translation, with the title *Legitimizing Architecture*, is held at IUAV-AP, De Carlo-scritti/095.

The English version of the article has been published on several occasions, under different titles and with some translation variants: "Legitimizing Architecture," *Forum* 23, no. 1 (1972): 8–21 (with the Dutch version alongside); "Architecture's Public," in Benedict Zucchi, *Giancarlo De Carlo* (Oxford, UK: Butterworth, 1992), 204–215; "Architecture's public," in Peter Blundell Jones, Doina Petrescu, and Jeremy Till (eds.), *Architecture and Participation* (London: Spon, 2005), 3–18.

Publisher contact:
The MIT Press
Massachusetts Institute of Technology
77 Massachusetts Avenue, Cambridge, MA 02139
mitpress.mit.edu

EU Authorised Representative:
Easy Access System Europe, Mustamäe tee 50,
10621 Tallinn, Estonia
gpsr.requests@easproject.com

Printed by Integrated Books International,
United States of America